Maggie Coat

Recognising Good Practice in Women's Education and Training

NIACE
THE NATIONAL ORGANISATION FOR ADULT LEARNING

Published by the National Institute of Adult Continuing Education
(England and Wales)
21 De Montfort Street, Leicester LE1 7GE

Company registration no. 2603322
Charity registration no. 1002775

First published 1996

Cover photograph by Stephen Leighton
Back cover photograph of NIACE Award Winners by Keith Ingley,
Ashley Colour Studios

Cataloguing in Publication Data
A CIP record for this title is available from the British Library

ISBN 1 872941 92 3

Printed in Great Britain by Antony Rowe Ltd, Chippenham, Wilts

Contents

Preface

NIACE: The National Organisation for Adult Learning has, on several occasions, made awards to both individual learners and learning providers in recognition of their achievements or to disseminate their work. NIACE's Women's Education Policy Committee (WEPC) was pleased to be invited in 1994 to make an award that specifically recognised Good Practice in Women's Education and Training.

In fact, the Committee decided to make six awards which would not only demonstrate good practice but also provide examples of some of the range of current educational and training provision for women – a range that recognises diversity and responds to difference. The Committee drew up a list of criteria against which provision would be judged and appointed a selection panel to examine the submissions against these criteria. The call for submissions was included in several editions of *Adults Learning* and was disseminated through existing networks.

Over 70 responses were received from a range of different types of providers, demonstrating diverse provision and coming from England and Wales, Scotland and Ireland. As we read through the submissions, it became apparent that most of them met the criteria – in fact almost all of them were examples of good practice.

Selecting the final six to whom awards were made was difficult and the so-called 'short list' grew longer and longer. Eventually, six very different kinds of provision were nominated.

Many of those who made submissions had already been recognised publicly as providers of good practice and were well established and well known; indeed some are known nationally, even internationally. Their claim to good practice cannot be doubted.

But the Committee decided to look for examples that clearly fulfilled all the criteria, were obviously well regarded and valued in their own locality or community, but may not have had the wider recognition they deserve. The selectors also looked for that something special in the submission – in the design of the provision – that not only makes it a good example of that particular kind of provision but distinguishes it from similar courses, centres or schemes.

Awards were made to:

- Awaaz Asian Women's Training Project in Sheffield
- Brush Up Your English and Maths, WEA East Midlands in Matlock
- Enterprising Women, WEA in the Highlands of Scotland
- Fresh Start Women's Access course, The Sheffield College
- Skills for Women provision based in Leeds
- Women's Safety Schemes that originated in Derby.

In March 1995, the six selected schemes received their awards at the NIACE WEPC Conference on International Women's Day in Birmingham. The theme of the conference was *Quality Issues in Women's Education and Training* and this seemed a suitable occasion to recognise the high quality of the six providers to whom awards were made.

NIACE's WEPC would like to thank all those who made submissions for the award and agreed that the material they submitted could be used in this publication. A list of all those who responded is included in Appendix 1. The book draws on many of these submissions and pays tribute to all those maintaining and developing good practice in women's education and training.

Acknowledgement

A sincere thank you to Geraldine Irving, who did most of the typing. Her help is much appreciated.

MAGGIE COATS
On behalf of the Women's Education Policy Committee of NIACE

Chapter 1

Introduction and Background

When NIACE's Women's Education Policy Committee (WEPC) were invited to make these awards, we had some reservations. We felt that by publicly recognising the work of a few providers we would be negating the value of others. While we believe that those to whom the awards were made on this occasion do represent good practice, we were very conscious that many of the submissions described provision of an equally high standard.

While we were pleased to recognise the work of the six providers and to disseminate their achievements, we were reluctant to ignore the very rich source of information on women's education and training represented by all those who made submissions. The detailed descriptions that had been sent gave us a great deal of evidence to show that women's education and training is still flourishing; that standards are high and, above all, that creativity and innovation were taking place, despite the current constraints and cut-backs. The WEPC felt that a publication should be prepared that would draw on the whole range of submissions and demonstrate the many facets of good practice. This book is an attempt to record and disseminate some of the work done by those who responded.

Even so we cannot include details of all the submissions nor reproduce all the material we were sent. Beyond asking for certain information, we had not indicated what form the submissions should take. Some completed the short proforma and attached a continuation sheet. Others wrote a fuller description of their work against the criteria we had given. We were also sent copies of proposals and reports, publicity material and evaluations. We received a book of student writing and a video. All of this we would like to disseminate more widely but it would be impossible to include it all in one book. To those whose course or scheme is not described or whose material is not used, we can only say that this does not imply that they do not demonstrate good practice but simply that we had a difficult choice.

However, the purpose of this book is not just to recognise and disseminate good practice but also to define it. In drawing up the criteria used to judge the submissions and make the awards, we had drawn on the experience of many women over many years of providing education and training opportunities for women (see Figure 1 below).

Figure 1. The criteria

Enabling criteria

- recruitment and access procedures that encourage the participation of women, particularly under-represented groups
- mechanisms to support and facilitate participation
- attention to students with special needs
- childcare provision or support
- low cost/concessionary fee policy
- learner support (including guidance and counselling)
- timing/location of provision to assist women with domestic commitments.

Responsiveness and transferability

- responsiveness to the needs of women
- responsiveness to the new funding mechanisms and structures to enable further development of good practice
- course design that is transferable to other learning contexts
- course design that includes potential for progression into employment, further or higher education or community activism.

Innovation and exploration

- innovation in the areas of curriculum, pedagogy and staff development.

Evaluation

- evidence of evaluation to monitor how effective the scheme/project/programme is and to identify ways in which it can change/evolve to meet women's needs.

Good practice has been described by NIACE and others on many occasions (Coats, 1993; McGivney, 1993; NIACE, 1991). The fact that so many submissions clearly met the criteria was an encouragement to us that as characteristics of good practice they were agreed and accepted but also that the criteria were clearly informing practice in a wide variety of situations. It was heartening to find that key components in provision for women that we had campaigned for over the years were now included as standard practice.

In publicising the awards we did not attempt to define what kinds of provision we expected to be included as 'women's education and training'; we accepted that in making submissions those who responded would anticipate that their provision should be included. However, the criteria did give some guidelines. For example, almost all the submissions describe provision for women who are currently unwaged but who are, or who may soon be, seeking to enter or re-enter education or training with the intention of returning to paid or self employment. Another assumption was that the provision would be primarily if not explicitly for *adult* women rather than younger women, although actual age is less significant than circumstances and experiences.

Less easy to decide is the extent to which the provision is designed explicitly and exclusively for women as opposed to being provision that is in fact open to all but attracts mainly women. We did not want to engage in a debate about provision that is women-only by design or by default, but the criteria made quite clear that the specific needs of women should be met. In fact, over 50 of the submissions described provision designed specifically for women.

Finally – and quite deliberately – we wanted to attract submissions from as diverse a range of provision as possible. In particular we welcomed examples that focused on the different needs of diverse groups of women – to celebrate difference and diversity. Our only concern was that what was being offered should particularly attract groups of women who are currently under-represented in either education or training. Again the interpretation of that must be related to specific circumstances and local need.

From the wide range of submissions we received it was apparent that there is indeed diversity in the groups for whom that provision is made, in the way it is delivered and in the content or curriculum included. In the following chapters, the submissions are described in broad categories, the rationale for which will be explained.

In addition to recognising the diversity of the submissions and the opportunity to share examples of good practice, it became apparent that several key issues were emerging from the material that gave us an insight into the way women's education and training is developing. The themes that constantly recurred have been identified, especially when they relate to changes in policy that are impacting directly on practice. Before summarising the categories of provision and including examples from the materials submitted, the next chapter isolates those themes and relates them to the current context in which women's education and training is provided. The concluding chapter returns to that context.

But before turning to the content of the submissions and the issues they raise, some reservations.

Limitations of this study

It is important to remember that the content of this book comes from submissions for an award and not from a survey of women's education and training. The contributors are self-selected in that they knew about the award – other good providers may not have done – and they decided to apply. Their submissions were written or compiled for that purpose and they did not originally expect to be making contributions to a book.

This point has to be remembered when examining the actual contributions. Some selections are taken from a short, straightforward application; others from a more lengthy submission. Some are extracts from documents compiled for other purposes; occasionally there is material from publicity leaflets. This means that there is no uniformity in the information given, and that a wide diversity of styles is used. In some cases extracts have been selected from what were much longer submissions.

The validity of the contributions and the analysis of them can also be questioned because all judgements, classifications and comments are based on *written* material produced and selected by the provider. It is impossible to judge the extent to which this translates into practice. We had originally hoped to short-list and visit some of the provision, but the numbers involved and the shortage of time made this impossible. Although evaluation evidence and supporting referees convinced us that the intentions and descriptions were translated into practice, we have no way of confirming this.

In addition, these submissions cannot be considered representative of the whole of women's education and training in Britain today, either in the type of provision and the numbers in each category or in geographical location. Indeed, as can be seen from the list in Appendix 1, the responses in each category and their distribution geographically is very uneven. The responses reflect both the readership of *Adults Learning* and, possibly, contacts with an organisation or national or regional network. Certain local clusters can be seen.

This, then, cannot give an overall picture of women's education and training but rather a snapshot – or album of snapshots – taken at one particular time. In effect all the responses arrived between June and October 1994.

Any interpretation of the response has to be seen in the light of all these reservations. Nevertheless, WEPC believed that there was much useful material here that should be shared. The selection of that material, its presentation and interpretation are the author's.

Chapter 2

Main Themes and Issues

The problem of classification

From the first examination of the materials submitted it was apparent that it was difficult to classify the provision described into clear categories or to distinguish between that which could be labelled as 'education' and that which could be identified as 'training'. This should come as no surprise to those who have been involved in women's education and training for some time, nor to those who have been affected by recent changes in policy and funding. The two categories have moved closed together and, in some cases, merged. (As they have in many areas of adult education provision.)

Indeed, in any good educational or training provision for women the components that ensure that the provision is appropriate must be present whatever the content or outcomes of that provision. There is a core of good practice within a diversity of forms. The fact that so many of the submissions showed clearly that they had met the stated criteria is added evidence of this; the criteria were intended to describe the characteristics by which good practice could be identified. Therefore it is likely that there will be common characteristics in both women's education and training that may make it difficult to differentiate between them.

One particular component of good practice has encouraged the distinction between education and training to be obscured, at least in practice. Many practitioners over the years have argued that for women returners the *outcomes* of the provision cannot be rigidly defined nor easily quantified. Because for many women it is a first step back into preparation for work or further education or training, many women will need time and space to explore the possible options. Prescribed exit routes may lead to inappropriate paths for some women. Personal growth and development may lead to a changed self-image or to alternative plans. Thus some women following a course of training in a specific skill area may find that their horizons are extended and other options become possible. It is well-documented that non-threatening, community-based women's groups have led many women to start on diverse paths to further education and training (McGivney, 1993).

But the other factor affecting the narrowing of the gap has undoubtedly been the vocationalising of some educational opportunities in an attempt to gain funding. This is not the place to explore this tendency in depth nor to analyse the cause of it more fully. The submissions endorse this trend but give no more than an indication of how this is happening in provision for women. It is demonstrated further in the attempt to categorise the submissions and in the chapters that include extracts from materials.

It is, however, interesting that many of the responses were from those who appeared to be offering *training* to women even though the readership of *Adults Learning* (where the awards were advertised) has traditionally been more firmly located in the 'educational' sector. And in terms of training opportunities for women the response is heavily skewed towards updating and training in areas that have traditionally and stereotypically been women's work. This in itself may represent an increase in this type of provision, particularly in FE colleges.

Providers and funders

The submissions were analysed in term of the providers, the funding sources and the accreditation offered to participants. This was a difficult task because providers were not asked for full details of this. Sometimes the person or organisation making the submission was not the provider; indeed one main point that emerged very clearly was that much of the provision was designed and delivered collaboratively. This is also reflected in the sources of funding. From the available evidence it appeared that of the 71 examples only 10 were funded from a single source, which, in most of those cases, was FEFC funding through a college.

Indeed, FE colleges were the main providers and the FEFCs the most frequently named source. Over half of the 71 received some or all of their funding under FEFC Schedule 2. But many of these also received some funding from the EC. We do not have full details of this but ESF and NOW sources were the most frequently mentioned.

For provision that is explicitly designed to assist women to return to work or to develop enterprise and self-employment opportunities there was evidence of some TEC funding; again the information is incomplete although there are quite detailed cases, some of which are included in Chapter 3. It might be added that, with one exception, there was little evidence of funding from commercial companies, although the Laura Ashley Foundation was mentioned in three submissions.

Other major providers and funders were various departments of local authorities. It was encouraging to see how often an adult education service or its equivalent was mentioned, sometimes with collaboration from another local authority department such as social services. Other sources were the final stages of urban programmes or urban aid and Section 11 money. There is no clear indication what will happen to this provision as these sources are removed.

Anyone who has been aware of developments in women's education over the last 20 or so years will not be surprised to learn that many submissions came from various branches of the WEA. As one of the original developers of the early 'New Opportunities for Women' courses, that WEA tradition is still strong but also changing. Some of the most innovatory programmes came from this organisation, which demonstrates how they have managed to merge provision that both encourages women to return to learning but also prepares for a return to paid work.

One other type of provision that takes a wide variety of forms was that designed to deliver education or training opportunities to women through women's centres or schemes. These include women's training centres specialising in the delivery of training in 'non-traditional' skills – such as manual skills, electronics and computing – as well as multi-purpose schemes that provide a range of services and opportunities for women, often covering a wide geographical area such as South Wales or Northern Ireland. Funding for these schemes still shows a balance between European sources and local authority departments, with some inputs from specific sources such as the Welsh Office.

Without doubt the most noticeable characteristic to emerge from the analyses of providers and of funding sources was the extent of collaboration and joint funding. Not surprisingly the most common was funding jointly from the EC and another source, which reflects the funding requirements. This led to examples of many kinds of interesting collaborative work, some of which is trans-national. However, at the other end of the scale was an example that named over 12 sources of funding and there were several with three, four or five different sources. What this reflects is the amount of work that must go into getting funding and how difficult it is to fund women's education; the possible conditions laid down by various funders; and the inevitable short-term nature, and therefore insecurity, of much of the provision. What is also evident from the submissions – and can be seen in many of the examples in the following chapters – is that the requirements of the funding source are making changes to the provision. There is a issue that perhaps needs raising here about how funding can, if largely from one source, skew provision away from original aims. This can be a problem if a scheme wishes to maintain integrity of purpose. This is most noticeable in terms of the insistence on accreditation.

The impact of accreditation

There has always been an expectation that some educational and training provision for women would lead to a recognised qualification. Courses for women leading to traditional 'academic' qualifications are well established; training for women that leads to a vocational qualification is not new. What has changed is the expectation that *most* provision for women would *not necessarily* lead to a qualification. This has always been an intentional part of the design of many providers – of informal learning opportunities and community-based work; of re-entry and threshold programmes; of courses designed to help women re-orient and explore options. Many of these, intentionally and for good reason, did not lead to certification of any kind. Veronica McGivney (1993) has argued well the case to retain and extend this kind of work.

The requirements imposed by funding regulations that insist that outcomes should be specified, progress assessed, individual participants certificated and the programme accredited has made a significant impact on all adult education and training, most particularly on that designed for women. Coupled with that has been the obvious move towards the vocationalisation of education so that the desired outcomes are either designated vocational qualifications or entry into the workforce.

This is an issue that needs to be explored more fully but which lies beyond the remit of this book. Sufficient to say that in the submissions for this award it is *the* most significant feature. It is significant because it is highly unlikely that had the material been collected five years ago, this would have emerged as an issue. From this material, however, its significance can be assessed in two ways – by examining the kind of accreditation which is evident and by exploring more carefully those kinds of provision where it is absent. This, however, is a major problem, because whilst the pro-forma accompanying the announcement of the award asked general details of funding, it made no explicit mention of accreditation.

What the criteria did expect, however, was evidence of:

> *responsiveness to the new funding mechanisms and structures to enable further development of good practice.*

Possibly because of this, or possibly because of its importance anyway, many providers who wrote more extensive submissions included details not just of funding but also of accreditation. What we were looking for in this case was evidence that if changes had been made in response to funding requirements – such as specified outcomes or accreditation – then the response to this should ensure that the characteristics of good practice are maintained. While it is not true that accreditation is necessarily undesirable – and there are strong arguments in favour of it – the emphasis is on what form it takes and how it is delivered.

Again, the form it takes is one of the major themes of this analysis in that 24 of the submissions made direct reference to accreditation through an Open College Network (OCN) – and indeed there may have been others who have OCN recognition but who did not include that information – while 16 providers mentioned NVQs. This confirms a pattern that is now becoming widespread in educational and training provision for women.

If it is considered appropriate to have some form of accreditation for provision and some form of certification for the women concerned – or if funding regulations require this – there is little doubt that the process of OCN recognition and the flexibility of that system is least likely to disrupt the essential components of the provision. Indeed OCN recognition is essentially recognition of the provision as it exists or as it is planned. The outcomes, the criteria for assessment and the evidence required are all determined by the provider with the support and advice of OCN staff; the essential nature of the provision can be retained. If a syllabus is imposed or the outcomes are prescribed, the provider has less control. The other major benefit of OCN recognition is that it can encompass a very wide range of learning programmes, both formal and informal; with academic, vocational or recreational content. It provides the learner with an opportunity to build up credits through further courses and to progress to higher levels. Many of the extracts in the following chapters make reference to the benefit of OCN recognition.

However, there are clearly some kinds of provision, particularly with a specific skills training input or occupational emphasis, where a recognised vocational qualification may enhance opportunities for progression or the employability of a participant. Women with considerable experience and skill but no formal qualifications who wish to enter or re-enter paid work may want to get a relevant NVQ (SVQ in Scotland) or other qualification. Also in evidence are a number of other awards – RSA CLAIT and other IT-related certificates; NEBSM courses; others from RSA and C&G; and SCOTVEC modules.

At the same time, there are concerns about the advisability of making provision for women to gain NVQs or other work-related qualifications that lead into a single occupational area, without providing sufficient advice and guidance about the implications of their choice and without the women having the opportunity to explore other options. This is particularly true of updating courses, where women who have been away from paid work for some time may not know what else is on offer nor realise what other skills they may have. Thus women remain in a narrow range of occupations that may confine them to a low paid job with little prospect of advancement. This is particularly true of some kinds of office employment and of work with children. On the other hand, if women have those skills and want that kind of employment, a recognised qualification may be important to them because it values those skills, gives public recognition to them and should improve their employment prospects.

Some reservations might also be voiced about encouraging women into non-traditional skills training where employment opportunities may now be limited. In terms of good practice, what is important is that the women make informed choices, that options are kept open and that any training or qualifications do lead to available work for women who need it.

In addition to provision that leads to OCN credits, and which can then lead to further progression in other forms of educational provision, within the submissions several other awards were mentioned – notably validated access to HE, certification in basic education such as Wordpower and Numberpower and, most interestingly, certificates in first aid. This confirms other evidence from colleagues in the field that there has been an increase in courses leading to a first aid qualification.

Because of the necessity of having to accredit provision to qualify for funding, and particularly to fit the requirements of the FEFC Schedule 2, there has always been concern that some provision that is not accredited, or that does not fit the categories designated in the schedule, will lose its funding and disappear. While we cannot be sure if the examples that do not mention accreditation are managing to get funding without it, it is significant that the group where this appears to be the case are those who provide the non-academic, non-vocational, re-entry provision. It would be useful to know more about this group and of how they are managing to survive.

Other important themes

Although issues of funding and accreditation appear to dominate the concerns of many who are providing education and training opportunities for women, other themes emerged from the submissions which were encouraging. The overall standard of the provision as demonstrated in the submissions and the apparent readiness to meet the criteria has already been mentioned; as indeed has the diversity of the provision even though a common core of good practice is identifiable. What emerged many times was the importance of designing provision to meet the needs of the *specific* groups of women who were being targeted. In the extracts there are many examples of provision for rural women as well as those confined to inner cities. There is provision specifically designed by and for Asian women, and for women of other ethnic minority groups, as well as instances where the needs of such women are recognised in provision for women of different backgrounds. There is evidence that good providers are ensuring that a range of options are available for *all* groups of women and that 'remedial' provision that leads nowhere is not acceptable. For example, there are several submissions where language support or help with basic education is part of a range of options provided alongside, or leading to, wider opportunities.

Another encouraging main theme is the inclusion of advice and guidance at all stages, leading to a variety of possible routes. Again the merging of education and training and the movement between each category can be discerned. Where providers included case studies of individual women it was not just linear progression or high level awards that were described, but increasing confidence to overcome obstacles and change direction was recognised as an important achievement.

Finally, among the submissions were a number that demonstrated the development of new ideas and innovative thinking. There were some that did not fall into a single category or group but bridged a whole range of types of provision on a large scale. There were others that though small-scale took an entirely new approach, recognising real needs and finding creative ways to respond. Within provision that seemed to fit a well-defined category or used well-tried programmes, there was evidence of new thinking and ways of meeting change. Even though most had a 'common core' that characterises good practice in provision for women, no two submissions were identical.

Thus selecting extracts to include in this book became as difficult as selecting the six award-winners. To make some sense of the themes and the patterns that emerged, I have classified the provision into three broad categories. Even here there is overlap and many could be placed in all three. Inclusion in any one does not mean that the provider sees that as the only or main outcome or that all the women concerned follow that route. I have used the categories to reflect the themes and to illustrate the diversity.

In Chapter 3, 'Return to Work', I have included a whole range of courses that lead many women towards or into paid employment or self-employment. Within it there are various sub-groups that look at different kinds of provision in this category.

Chapter 4 focuses on 'Return to Learn', where the emphasis is not on preparation for employment as such but on giving women opportunities to take up learning at whatever level and in whatever context is appropriate for them. Rather than sub-groups, this category has overlapping areas of concern and different ways of providing leaning in response to a range of needs.

The next chapter, as the title 'Return to Re-assess' implies, contains a collection of examples that allow women to choose from a variety of types of provision or to spend time discovering which might be most appropriate for them. Further sub-sections look at two other types of provision, equally difficult to classify, one of which focuses on re-entry through childcare and parenting, while the final group contains the new or innovative provision that does not fit any other description.

The book ends with a chapter that returns to the issues which have been raised and to the lessons we have learned from the submissions to the Good Practice awards, poses some important questions and draws some conclusions.

Chapter 3

Return to Work Provision

3.1 General return to work and updating courses

Of the 71 submissions for the award, 14 could be placed in this category. Given the means by which the award was publicised, this is a high response, but it reflects all the indications that work-related provision is expanding. Not surprisingly, this reflects both funding and accreditation requirements.

Most of the provision in this category came from FE colleges, often using joint FEFC and ESF funding. Of all the categories, this was the one with the most examples of funding from TECs. This was also the category where outcomes related to NVQs were most common, with RSA qualifications, particularly CLAIT, in evidence.

The submissions in this category fall into two groups:

(a) those with wide options for progression and a very general 'return to work' input

(b) those that contained a specific occupational input.

In group (a) there were examples from a wide range of locations, both urban and rural. Most of this provision gives women a choice of progression routes. In group (b) the choice was narrower, with many courses including some form of business administration, office skills and information technology.

This was particularly true of the updating courses. For example, the most common NVQ associated with these courses was Business Administration. Many had an IT component, although much of the content is related to office work.

3.1.1 Women on the Move

SURREY ADULT CONTINUING EDUCATION

The purpose of this project is to enable women returners to re-enter the job market at a level that is appropriate to their abilities, skills and experience. Funding for this project is not output-related. It has therefore been possible to develop a learning environment to match individual and group needs. This empowers the participants in groups and individually to negotiate their programme. A holistic approach is taken, developing personal and marketable skills alongside longer-term career planning that may include return to study. Personal targets are so often missing for those whose role has been to care for others. Participants gain accreditation for current competence by providing evidence against national standards,using unpaid work either at home or in the community or administering their own programme.

Enabling criteria

Recruitment and access procedures

Positive action is taken to attract women who are isolated within the community, ethnic minorities, women who have been restricted in their ability to take up training opportunities because of their caring responsibilities and/or women from low income families who traditionally do not attend fee paying training courses. Publicity was translated into five languages that reflected the mix of local population. Press articles and advertisements were placed and leaflets supplied to Job Centres, CAB, Careers Service and voluntary organisations working with women. Information events were held, after which every applicant received a personal interview to discuss the programme and whether it would match their perceived needs.

Mechanisms to facilitate and support participation

- Final offers of a place were determined by the match of student need and recruitment criteria, which were that participants must be over 25 years old and out of full-time paid work for three years or more.
- The complete course, including childcare, was free to participants.

- Advice and counselling aimed at improving self-image and confidence is provided on career choices and training opportunities; applications for work and/or FE/HE courses; self-auditing and preparation of portfolios for APEL; preparation for assessment for NVQ units. Much informal advice is available and some specific individual time is built into the programme.
- The programme is offered during term-time only for 13 weeks, 9.30 am to 2.30 pm, five days a week, to build up commitment and peer group support. The course has now been held in four different locations across the county, in urban and rural areas. This brings the course to the women and reduces their expense and travelling time.

Responsiveness and transferability

Needs of women

Personal confidence and self-image can have a profound effect on the way women re-enter the job market after a period out of paid work. Despite having the ability, skills, and experience, most women returners lack the confidence to apply for a range of jobs. This project has at its core a training programme designed to develop confidence, decision-making, job and education search skills, and to offer current qualifications.

Funding

The project is supported by Surrey County Council and the European Social Fund (ESF). It has enabled Surrey Adult Continuing Education service to draw on several facets of its traditional programme and integrate them with new developments and forms of assessment.

Course design and transferability

The programme is aimed at entry into employment, with a foundation of administration and information technology skills. Extra OCN accreditation has been added during the life of the project to recognise the importance of study skills. Students complete an initial introduction to option modules before specialising after week four of the programme.

Main components

- personal development
- career options and job search skills
- information technology (RSA)
- health and safety at work (NVQ)
- portfolio development (OCN)

Options

- return to study (OCN)
- business administration (NVQ)
- core text skills (RSA)
- maths and English workshops.

APEL accreditation at NVQ levels 2/3 recognises experiential learning and transferable skills both in participants' everyday lives and on the course.

Innovation and exploration

Curriculum innovations

- integration of the disciplines
- involvement of students in administering aspects of the programme, for example student-led decisions about content and the organisation of outside contributions from specialist speakers and employers, fostering of teamwork in co-ordinating the arrangements for visiting speakers and chairing sessions.

Pedagogy

- a facilitative style of teaching drawing on existing abilities
- building a learning environment that enabled students to experience challenge and achievement
- use of active learning techniques
- tutors' understanding and empathy with students (most of the tutors have experienced a career break).

Staff development

- development of awareness of the complete programme and how elements informed the assessment for NVQ and Open College credits
- development of team-teaching and cross-curricular skills

- awareness of process of advice and assessment for NVQ and practice leading to accreditation for D32, 33 and 36 (the NVQ assessor units)
- development of interview techniques, advice and guidance skills
- setting up of administrative systems to suit the needs of funding providers.

Evaluation

Monitoring effectiveness

- students involved in structured feedback sessions as groups and individuals
- records of progress on and after the course are maintained
- regular team meetings of programme managers and tutors
- external accreditation and moderation as a measure of quality standards.

Evolving to meet women's needs

The programme is designed by women for women to fill the gap in the local education and training provision. For returners 9.30 am to 2.30 pm is a full day, whereas most providers were offering inflexible 9.00 am to 5.00 pm courses. Coping successfully with a five-hour day gave some students the confidence to apply for and obtain full-time work

These changes were made following evaluation:

- information and induction period (four weeks) modified after the first cohort of student and tutor evaluation
- the approach to NVQs and portfolio work. This includes all students doing one unit on health and safety and an essay before choosing their options
- OCN accreditation of the return to study module has been added.

3.1.2 Women's Retraining Projects

ROTHER VALLEY COLLEGE

These are based at Swallownest Youth Centre, Kiveton Youth Centre and Thurcroft Welfare Hall. This provision began under the

Rotherham Women's Training Group initiative, whose initial aims were:

- to meet the educational needs of women who wish to return to paid employment after a time spent raising a family
- to benefit women who do not have ready access to retraining at the main college site
- to benefit women who live in relatively isolated communities
- to benefit women from communities suffering economic and social deprivation, whose confidence and aspirations are low and who initially perceive a course of retraining as a threatening rather than rewarding experience
- to enable women students to gain confidence in job seeking, to develop career/life plans that positively reflect their abilities and aptitude.

The aims have not changed but have been slightly readjusted to take account of the changing realities of employment that have altered the basic economies of more local communities.

Aims

- to address the educational needs/provision of women in the college catchment areas, taking into account women's roles, lifestyle, constraints and family responsibilities and commitments
- to address the access issues and barriers to participation such as lack of finance, safety, the need for an empathetic learning environment and good on-site childcare provision
- to address the need for provision in local premises
- to address the issues of fee levels and enrolment costs
- to accredit women's skills and achievements in a nationally recognised format
- to make the content relevant and appropriate in order to encourage a review of values, skills and experiences and so enable these to be located in a wider context
- to offer educational guidance and support on-site to raise awareness of local employment possibilities and progression routes

- to provide vocational guidance in a variety of forms, e.g. International Women's Day celebrations, College Open Days, etc.

Funding was achieved through the Vocational Guidance sub-committee that bids to the ESF for funds to support these activities at college and makes possible the women's attendance by providing transport and on-site childcare.

Objectives

- to bid for funding to the European Social Fund (ESF) to enable free access and provision
- to provide free on-site childcare support that is integral to the bid
- to bid with Youth Service, local authority and community management teams to provide appropriate local venues for delivery
- to write submissions when necessary to SYOC for learning programmes (Personal Effectiveness). All other areas of accreditation are sited in nationally recognised qualifications. Programmes are negotiated with students within the limits of what is available on each site, staffing availability and resources
- to continuously recognise the necessity to update the educational provision in line with student needs and the needs of the local economy
- to offer personal tutorial time and on-site support from the Educational Guidance Service for Adults. Students are invited to participate in free educational activities and vocational guidance, visits and residential weekends.

Description of programme

The three core skill areas of computer work, personal effectiveness and return to study, maths and English are negotiated with students from the list below:

- SYOC Personal Effectiveness
- RSA Typewriting I/II
- RSA Wordprocessing I/II
- RSA CLAIT

- RSA Book-keeping/Accounts
- RSA Spelltest
- RSA English
- City and Guilds Numeracy I/II/III/IV 3750
- City and Guilds Wordpower I/II 3793.

Mode of delivery

Individual tuition within group learning sessions tailored to suit individual levels of requirement. Supported self-study is essential to the programme.

Completion/progression

Student progression routes include access to Higher Education, other vocationally related courses both at this college and elsewhere, employment and voluntary sector work.

3.1.3 Women Into Work

SOUTH LEEDS OPEN LEARNING CENTRE

Background

Women Into Work was developed in response to needs of women in socially deprived inner city areas in Leeds. Many women have not participated in post-16 education and training, have no formal qualifications and do not see traditional adult education as relevant to their needs. Approximately 10 per cent of the community are from ethnic minorities. These women have many skills but, caught in a poverty trap, have low self-confidence and self-image and feel unable to aim high. In many cases they do not have the information and guidance necessary for progression. The only jobs available are 'dead-end', with little security, low pay and few prospects.

There are support groups and workers providing an excellent service in the community. However, for most women a central site college course is not an option because of its physical and perceptual remoteness. There is an overwhelming need for local, well-resourced, substantial courses providing the support and skills to move confidently into work or further education/training. Courses need to be manageably short, sufficiently relevant to work aims, and to offer achievable short-term goals.

Women Into Work is designed to meet this 'interim step' need with recognised qualifications and development of self-worth and transferable skills.

The course aims to build confidence and skills in a small, supportive group. It runs simultaneously on two sites, both serving communities with high unemployment and social disadvantage and little opportunity to move out of the poverty trap.

Description

Core programme (12 hours a week for 10 weeks):

- basic IT awareness (women who are computer literate are offered an alternative)
- team leadership/supervisory skills
- wider opportunities and job search skills
- health, safety and emergency aid at work
- confidence building and assertiveness
- communication skills
- psychology of work/women and power

Options:

- introduction to caring
- European language taster
- art and design
- work experience
- creative writing
- residential week at Northern College – women in society
- brush up your skills – maths and English workshop.

Open Learning Centres are available throughout the week for flexible support with study skills, maths, English, Computing and keyboard skills. There are regular tutorials; advice and guidance; benefit and rights advice; and ESOL support.

The course is accredited through the National Examining Board for Supervisory Management (Introductory Certificate for Women), St John's Ambulance and Open College. There are opportunities to work towards RSA Computer Literacy and City and Guilds Numeracy certificates.

Innovation

We believe the programme to be particularly innovative in the following respects:

1. The course offers the opportunity to gain a recognised qualification in the context of a much broader, supportive curriculum that extends skills and interests.
2. The degree of support for women taking an initial step back into work, training or education. The programme reflects the ethnic profile of the community and has proved attractive to previous non-participant groups (70 per cent were new to adult education).
3. Running at two sites simultaneously has facilitated staff development and group interaction. Given continued funding the course will be offered at different, suitably equipped sites in the community.
4. Partnerships: Park Lane College in partnership with the WEA secured European funding which enabled us to offer a broad-ranging programme with progression roots and benefit from a cross-fertilisation of ideas. We are seeking a wider European dimension with the European languages, a module on European issues, and, we hope, exchange work experience and socio-political visits.
5. The range of learning methods allows students to develop independence of learning and select preferred modes of study.

Criteria

Enabling

Wide publicity through schools, nurseries and women's groups. Publicity was also disseminated through existing and new networks of agencies in the community. The course has been successful in recruiting from the target groups. Course times are designed to fit with the school day and a well-equipped, professionally-staffed crèche is available. Advice, guidance and workshop support are freely available. The course is free and a small subsistence allowance is paid to participants.

Women Into Work runs in the communities it seeks to serve. The course includes a day at the main site college with children using the crèche facilities; an introduction to college services and Learning Resource Centre; use of the excellent careers section; and advice on grants and benefits. Part of the aim of the day is to make progression seem more accessible.

Responsiveness and transferability

The course has fulfilled its aims of increasing confidence and communication skills linked with a recognition of existing strengths that has enabled outstanding progression and outcomes. Women have moved into vocational education and training, further education, community work and employment at junior supervisory level. All of the women have taken up new opportunities and are now very highly motivated.

All participants recognise their ability to achieve at a much higher level, their abilities and strengths, and the transferability of prior experience.

The course is flexible and pro-active, with 'discovery' of how teams function, leadership and organisational skills.

Evaluation

Students are fully involved in evaluation of materials, learning/teaching methods, individual modules and the course as an entity. There are regular staff meetings and cross-centre co-ordination. The team is fully informed of student comments in order to plan and deliver a relevant, responsive course.

Students are encouraged to take part in the Centre Users' Group and thus to influence general policy and planning.

The programme has included a most successful 'Introduction to Caring Services' option that can lead to flexible learning GNVQs in health and social care at both Centres. We are also investigating the wider perspective of a substantial European link with a European studies module and a visit to Brussels. In response to student feedback we have extended the length of the psychology module and included the option of Open College accreditation for this unit.

3.1.4 Pathways for Women Returners

LLANDRILLO COLLEGE, CLWYD

This free programme is designed specifically for women who wish to re-enter the labour market and takes into account both past and future economic trends in the area. Due to the types of job that have been traditionally available to women – service industries, the retail trade and caring sectors – women have suffered both horizontal and vertical occupational segregation.

In an attempt to redress this balance the course has a high content of personal development aimed at improving women's self-image and teaching them to aspire. It seeks to empower participants to make better choices about their futures by enabling them to become better choosers. The course also aims to provide women with both generic and specific skills to meet the needs of a changing economy and to encourage women to seek employment in areas where feminisation of occupations/wages has not yet taken place.

Attracting students from a wide range of socio-economic groups, the course seeks to address the differences of participants' experiences and abilities by using differentiation in the learning environment in a positive and structured way. In addition the programme offers vocational tasters in all areas of the curriculum, positively promoting progression routes and credit accumulation for APEL purposes. It aims to look at the validity and transferability of skills and to contextualise these within the paid working environment.

This geographical catchment area spans areas of urban deprivation on the coast and agricultural decline in the rural setting, together with the issue of a bi-lingual community. In this setting the programme is provided within a climate of socio-economic regeneration. Employment opportunities are often new and different from those traditional to the area. In this we seek to work with employers and enterprise agencies to ensure a new philosophy and ethos towards flexible patterns of work. Responsiveness to this is central to the programme to ensure that participants are not only aware of developments but are equipped to aspire and succeed in a changing labour market.

The Chwarae Teg Initiative was set up in early 1992 in South Wales, and extended in May 1993 to North and Mid Wales following two major research projects undertaken by the Welsh Development Agency and a group of public sector employers.

The research sought to examine the reasons why Wales has the lowest rate of female participation in paid work of any region in the UK; it aimed to examine the barriers and constraints that exist for women entering or re-entering the workforce or who wish to access training.

It is well known that women who have been out of the workforce for sometimes prolonged periods of time often experience problems when the time comes to reassess their lives. Many women feel a lack of confidence, a loss of self-belief and a sense of isolation when they have been confined to a domestic role for an extended period. They often feel that their skills, qualifications and experience are out-dated.

Our research identified that much of the training available in Wales is not geared to meet these women's needs; that what is required are flexible, women-only courses that will help students to build self-confidence, recognise and value their individual skills and achievements and assist them in identifying routes for further progression to enable them to make informed choices about their future personal development.

The Pathways for Women programme is an excellent example of this model, designed to meet all the above criteria.

3.1.5 Returning to Work, Further Education or Training

NENE VALLEY ADULT EDUCATION, NORTHANTS

Aim and nature

To enable women living in rural East Northants to gain the confidence and skills to return to appropriate employment, education or training after an absence from the labour market.

A preparatory course held in a rural location, e.g. village hall, for 12 women. Completion by attendance three mornings per week or a mixture of attendance and tutor-supported home study.

Course components: review/evaluation of experience to date – exploration of own potential – preparation of portfolio of experience and CV – evaluation of local employment/training opportunities, self-employment and voluntary work – communication skills

– problem-solving – decision-making skills – assertiveness – job-seeking skills – application and interview skills – basic skills refresher – financial planning – introduction to IT.

Good/innovative practice

Enabling criteria

- recruitment: women only who have not been in regular employment for the last year. Women with physical or learning disabilities are integrated within the group. Attention is paid to selection of accessible venues. Where more than 12 women wish to participate, every effort is made to accommodate them
- childcare costs are met and help is given with finding childminders. Playgroups are not always available in villages and village premises can rarely support a course-plus-crèche
- travel costs are reimbursed – including taxi fares where there is no other possible transport
- courses are free to participants
- educational and vocational guidance and counselling is offered as an integral part of the course by both course tutors and a guidance worker
- additional basic skills support is available through a basic education programme
- courses are timed to allow women to drop children at school/playgroup/childminder in the morning and collect at lunchtime. The option to complete parts of the course by supported home study gives greater flexibility. Use of local village halls or community organisation premises brings opportunities closer to women who are isolated in a rural area.

Responsiveness and transferability

- within the course components there is the flexibility to meet the needs of individual women
- feedback indicates that women find the course meets their needs
- in order to respond to funding mechanisms and promote progression, the course has been reviewed, extended to 120

hours and submitted to Buckinghamshire Open College for recognition. This will allow women to gain up to four credits at Level 2 or 3

- the model of curriculum and delivery has proved successful and provoked interest among other groups. A similar style of course is now being piloted in a village in North East Northants specifically for people with physical disabilities
- the course promotes progression to further education, training or employment, or involvement in voluntary work and community projects. Open College accreditation enhances this. Women have progressed to:
  - employment
  - self-employment
  - voluntary work
  - further education, including Access courses, GCSEs, NVQs, etc.
  - higher education, e.g. teacher training, degree courses
  - part-time adult education, e.g. RSA CLAIT, basic skills, office skills, GCSEs and other learning for personal development.
- a support network has been set up on a self-help basis, with assistance from an outreach worker, to maintain contact, mutual support and motivation.

Innovation and exploration

- completion by attendance or a mixture of attendance and home study
- visits of course members to local employers and colleges
- involvement of returners who have succeeded in returning to work or achieved their goals in education/training.

Evaluation

- a clear set of aims, objectives and anticipated learning outcomes against which the course is measured by managers, tutors and the women themselves
- the views of participants are sought during the course in discussions, both as a group or one-to-one. Peer and self-assessment against learning outcomes is encouraged

- trainers present written reports at the end of the course including a summary of course evaluation by the women. Reports are made regularly to the Governors of Nene Valley Adult Education
- Changes are made to the course (e.g. recent change in hours, development of accreditation) to respond to women's needs
- staff development needs are met as identified, e.g. in relation to nature and use of formal accreditation.

3.1.6 New Start

SAXMUNDHAM MIDDLE SCHOOL

Rationale

Women living in rural areas are doubly disadvantaged in accessing opportunities to return to work or study. Courses, projects and advice are concentrated in urban areas and already inaccessible to anyone who is financially, socially, educationally disadvantaged or not ready or able to return to full-time employment immediately. In addition rural people face transport, time and proportionately more childcare/dependant costs. The 'New Start Project is a community-based project to enhance the educational, economic and social development of a rural area.

Aims

The aim of the project is to provide an appropriate, well-equipped setting that values rural people, and their specific needs, and enables women and other disadvantaged people to update or learn new skills, provide life choices, develop confidence and work at their own pace in an informal, non-competitive environment. Courses fit the needs of individuals and provide the following advantages not available in traditional training: no time limit for attending, affordable price, free childcare, free transport, individual attention, examinations when student feels ready, on-going personal support, educational guidance, careers guidance.

Objectives

To provide accessible, affordable courses in office skills, computer/information technology, typing, word-processing, business communication, book-keeping, inter-personal skills, small business management in year one.

To target services at disadvantaged groups, e.g. women, people with physical disability, people with learning disability, people recovering from mental illness.

To enable people to gain the knowledge, skills, attitudes necessary to enable them to have choices. Choices could include return to work/study, taking examinations, accessing their community, volunteering, gaining confidence.

Years two/three to provide a community/business resource similar to a telecottage.

Further points

New Start is different from other training because it is community-based within a rural area and because it is aimed specifically at women.

It provides opportunities for women to gain knowledge, attitudes and skills that can prepare them for employment, allow them to change direction, return to work or study, increase their community involvement, support their volunteering or simply give opportunities for personal development and increased independence and life choices.

Skills-based training is offered in business administration, computing, information technology, typewriting, word processing, business communication, book-keeping, audio, inter-personal skills. Short courses and workshops can be offered in interview skills, spelling, writing CVs, health and safety. The Careers Service offers Stepping Stones courses and Jobsearch.

New Start is accessible, social, comfortable and very well equipped with modern technology.

Courses fit the needs of individuals. People work at their own pace in an informal, friendly, non-competitive environment. qualifications can be taken when people feel ready. On-going personal support, careers and education guidance is given.

It removes the blocks traditionally associated with women returning by being flexible (courses can be full- or part-time), operating women-friendly hours (10.00 am to 3.00 pm, or evenings), keeping fees low, under-writing childcare and transport costs.

New Start is supported by Suffolk County Council Community Education, Suffolk Training and Enterprise Council, Rural Development Commission, Suffolk Coastal District Council.

Flexible session-times allow for evening or weekend spaces to be made available to local businesses and organisations for training courses based on their particular needs.

3.1.7 Women Returners – Information Technology

CITY OF LIVERPOOL COMMUNITY COLLEGE

The Women Returners IT Project is in its final year of support from a three-year Urban Aid Project Grant. It has offered hundreds of women accreditation and progression opportunities in word-processing, spreadsheets and databases. This year we are introducing electronics and video technology.

We have purchased 30 high-quality laptop computers and 10 printers. Each day staff collect the machines from main college centres and work throughout the local community with women who for various reasons can not yet come into college but require education and training.

We have designed the programme to fit in with the needs of women returners, and linking up with other community projects has ensured that childminding is available to women on our courses.

Qualifications range from basic skills accreditation to CLAIT. Link-up with the college's computer terminal has been made to ease progression onto both vocational and academic mainstream courses.

This year we are providing NVQs and we will introduce electronics and video technology as options for women on the project.

IT can be the main subject for outreach students or it can be a core subject on a broader programme. Links are being made between our women returners project and another course the college offers on an outreach basis – New Opportunities for Women.

We will embed the women returners IT project by integrating the technological elements we have developed with other programmes we offer through outreach.

We believe that the success of the project so far has depended on the quality of the staff, equipment and services we offer. We employ highly trained female staff to teach IT to women in a non-traditional setting. This learning facility is not otherwise available in the community.

Our recruitment, retention, accreditation and progression records are excellent, which proves that we have succeeded in building confidence to achieve and quality in content.

3.1.8 Women Into Office Administration and New Technology

DONCASTER COLLEGE

Aims and nature of the course

The course is funded by the European Social Fund (ESF), which means the fees are waived for every student. Provision is also made for examination fees to be paid and for a student residential fee. However, there are no cash bonuses and for some students childcare provision and transport are a problem. With the advent of Training for Work (TFW), we made available the option whereby they can still claim Income Support and have their bus fares paid and obtain money for childminding. A few students choose this option.

The timetables are fixed around the hours of 10.00 am to 3.00 pm and the location of the beginners' course is in central Doncaster. Two beginners' classes are running at present. These last for about 16 weeks and then students may progress to the advanced course. The Course Tutor offers an hour's tutorial every week where any problems can be shared.

Early on in the course both beginners' classes enjoy a residential weekend at High Melton. Assertiveness and confidence-building are the themes of the weekend. Students get to know each other better and have a good time too.

Whereas on the beginners' course the emphasis is on updating skills and confidence building, on the advanced course we concentrate on more academic skills. This year, for the first time, we have been accredited by the National Examining Board in Supervisory Management (NEBSM). On the beginners' course students obtain the NEBSM Introductory Certificate on successful completion of the communications and finance modules. On the advanced course students add book-keeping, Spanish, law, supervising people, interviewing and a project to these modules in order to obtain the full NEBSM certificate. Studying more academic subjects raises the students' aspirations.

Students on the beginners' course also undertake a two-week work-placement which they find for themselves. Letters of application are written in the communications class. We are building up a good reputation amongst employers and several students have been offered jobs. One woman in her 50s gained employment at the hospital following a placement there. The Educational Guidance Officer talks to students, and some progress to further education.

Course Team Meetings and students' complaints are taken very seriously. The first time the course was run we had databases, spreadsheets and word processing all in the same week. After students voiced their confusion, we now teach the subjects in separate modules, leaving word processing until last, when students have had time to gain or improve keyboard skills. This year we have put three extra hours of NVQ support onto the timetable because students wanted it. The advanced course that was run last year was a mere extension of the beginners' course and we had a large drop-out rate, hence the restructuring into the present successful NEBSM form.

Students on the advanced course are busy at present fund-raising for a proposed work-placement in Barcelona – which explains the Spanish on the timetable.

3.1.9 MATREC NVQ Embedding Project

MANOR TRAINING AND RESOURCE CENTRE, SHEFFIELD

Manor Training and Resource Centre (MaTReC) is a voluntary sector training and educational project situated on the Manor in Sheffield. An inner city estate of some 13,000 people, Manor is one of Sheffield's deprived and disadvantaged areas.

MaTReC was one of the first organisations to run South Yorkshire Open College Federation (SYOCF) accredited courses in 1987.

Since 1990 the project has run a Complete Office programme designed to get long-term unemployed Manor people back into work. Modules include basic English and maths, basic computers, computers 2, book-keeping, typing, wordprocessing, office skills and jobsearch. All modules are accredited by SYOCF.

In October 1992 we were part of a feasibility study – conducted by SYOCF and funded by Sheffield TEC – that explored ways of embedding access to assessment for NVQs in business administration into our SYOCF accredited Complete Office programme. As an outcome of this, we embedded access to the full NVQs at levels 1 and 2.

Although the programme is not exclusively aimed at women, the participants on our NVQ Business Administration programme thus far have all been female. Clearly we are facilitating access to nationally recognised qualifications for a group of often marginalised disadvantaged women returners.

There are no costs attached to our NVQ provision. We also run a free crèche to enable women with young children to attend. We offer ongoing counselling and support.

Strengths of the embedding method

The programme offers a high degree of flexibility, catering for a diverse range of student aptitudes, needs and preferences. For some students, for example, the need to learn in a friendly, comfortable environment may be of primary importance. Here SYOCF accreditation is paramount. Others might be sufficiently confident in their own abilities to produce hard outcomes and carry out valuable work for the project in the process.

Embedding means that NVQs are implicit. This is very important for an organisation like MaTReC that is endeavouring to develop methods of improving access in an area where most people failed in their first attempt at education and are consequently disillusioned with mainstream forms of education and training. The system we have adopted means that trainees are able to access NVQs in the process of undertaking NOCN provision.

The fact that we can retain SYOCF and not abandon it altogether was also important for our tutors for it enabled them to evolve gradually into new areas.

The embedding process merges the strengths of a learning-based approach with a harder-edged outcome-based system. We have called this the development of a 'seamless theoretical and practical experience in a living environment in which learning and work are totally compatible and mutually interchangeable'. This may sound a little grand, but what it means is that students learn and work, and work and learn, in a fluid environment.

The other important aspect of this project is the potential that NVQs are realising in revitalising the local community.

NVQs and socially beneficial work

When we embarked on the project we saw the potential for using NVQs as a direct stimulus for socially useful and constructive work in the community.

This has certainly been put into practice. One woman, for example, was commissioned to carry out a comparative study of qualification rates at MaTReC and two Sheffield College centres. When we first formulated the objectives of the project we identified five positive outcomes as a result of such audits. These were:

- a good learning experience for students
- a good work experience for students
- achievement of accreditation
- combining business administration with social education; students could arrive at a clearer, more self-conscious understanding of what factors, for example, affect their participation in training and education
- useful information for MaTReC and for other training organisations working in the community.

The quality of the work/learn experience

MaTReC prides itself on being a 'transparent' organisation. What this means is that NVQ students are actively encouraged to carry out all aspects of the project's day-to-day organisation and administration, including handling its financial work. This kind of unrestricted work experience for candidates not only equips them for work, but also gives them a moral and social education, for it enables them to be an essential part of a constructive community initiative.

Accreditation of Prior Achievement (APA)

We also envisaged the possibilities of APA in opening up the latent potential that many local people possessed. We saw APA, by being synonymous with easily accessible accreditation, as being, ironically, a spur to people to undertake formal training. In other words, being recognised for the skills they already possessed would encourage people to want to gain more skills and qualifications. This process was deemed integral to our aim of evolving a qualifications culture in an area of high unemployment and educational under-achievement.

We have offered APA on a regular basis, and this is a growing aspect of our work.

Conclusion

There are now 40 people on the NVQ Business Administration programme. Clearly, it is becoming increasingly popular. Allied to this, more and more people from various organisations and agencies are visiting our Centre to look at the programme and how it is delivered. It is being widely seen as a pioneering approach to the delivery of NVQs to long-term unemployed and unwaged adults living on a deprived inner-city estate.

3.2 Training in non-traditional skill areas

Information technology also figured in some of the non-traditional return to work provision. Of all the categories this was the one where the response was least representative of the provision available. This may be due to the ways in which the award was publicised and to the perceived emphasis on 'education' rather than training. The work of the Women's Training Network which co-ordinates and campaigns on behalf of schemes offering training in non-traditional skills areas shows that there are still many opportunities for women to train through this type of provision. This is the sector that has most directly benefited from EC funding. Of the five submissions we received, all except one received joint ESF/FEFC or ESF/local authority funding. Two of them were well-known schemes of long standing whose work has been recognised both nationally and internationally on many occasions. The other two were courses located in colleges that provided more focused provision in a single skill area. However, there was one submission in this category that did not relate directly to returning to work in a non-traditional skill area but which set out to encourage women to consider a range of possible routes through courses with a science or technology base. These are areas where women are still in a minority and this course sets out to demystify these subjects for women returners.

3.2.1 South Glamorgan Women's Workshop

CARDIFF

Aims and nature of the scheme

South Glamorgan women's workshop is a new technology training initiative for women, currently financed by the European Social Fund, South Glamorgan County Council and Vale of Glamorgan Borough Council. It aims to provide vocational training of the highest quality to unemployed women, enabling them to develop the technical and personal skills necessary to re-enter employment, thereby leading to greater economic independence and social well-being. The current daytime course in business computing and Computer Networking leads to City & Guilds 7261 qualifications in business and office technology and information technology NVQ Level 2, and the Workshop is seeking to accredit the non-technical aspects of the course via the Open College Network.

Expertise developed during the Workshop's 10 years of existence enables it to provide the key elements recognised for successful training of women.

These elements include:

- free training on daytime courses
- travel expenses reimbursed
- situated close to bus and train stations
- courses run to correspond with school terms and times
- on-site childcare by trained professional staff
- an introductory course for ethnic minority women
- a City & Guilds mathematics course to give confidence in numeracy
- complementary studies, e.g. study and communication skills, literacy and confidence-building, job-seeking and interview skills
- liaison with employers for visits, placements and relevance of training to labour market needs
- work experience providing an opportunity for trainees to see how technology is used and to try out new skills in a real working environment
- advice and guidance enabling women to make informed choices for further or higher education, training or employment
- counselling to assist women balance the demands of training or work and family responsibilities.

Facilities at the Workshop are maximised by the development of a self-financing Short Course Programme that enables women not eligible for daytime courses to update both their technical and personal skills. In addition, local employers may further benefit from flexible in-house training provided by short course tutors covering a wide range of business packages and complementary topics that assist progression in employment.

The Workshop has endeavoured to keep abreast of changes in technology, women's training needs and employers' skills needs. In addition, every effort is made to update equipment and resources and to provide staff training and development so that the Workshop remains at the forefront of women's training. It has recently been approved as an Information Technology NVQ Training Centre. All teaching staff are in the process of gaining appropriate NVQ qualifications.

As a European Social Fund project with matched funding from local authorities, evaluation is an essential activity. An early evaluation of the Workshop, *New Styles of Training for Women*, was commissioned by the Equal Opportunities Commission and published in 1986. A full audit of the Workshop was undertaken by the Department of Employment on behalf of the European Commission in October 1992. An innovative course in telematics and telecommunications was trialled at the Workshop in 1992/3 and 1993/4 and has been comprehensively evaluated by CREW, the Co-ordinator for the European Commission's NOW programme. In addition, the Workshop has featured in numerous publications as an exemplar of good practice and continues to be consulted on all aspects of successful training for women.

South Glamorgan Women's Workshop has trained more than 2,500 women since 1984, providing them with new skills needed for today's world of work. It will continue to strive to provide vocational training of the highest quality that balances the needs of both women and local employers.

3.2.2 Women's Education In Building

CONSTRUCTION SKILLS TRAINING CENTRE, LONDON

Women's Education in Building (WEB) was founded in 1984 and since that time has grown to become Europe's largest construction industry training centre for women. The women we train are all long-term unemployed adults, the majority are from ethnic minorities, most are lone parents and few have had any post-secondary education or further training.

We provide training in six major trades, carpentry, plumbing, bricklaying, plastering, painting and decorating, and electrical installation to City & Guilds and NVQ standards.

WEB is a voluntary organisation dedicated in providing opportunity where there is so little for adult women. We are also an organisation whose track-record speaks for itself. On average over 80 per cent of our trainees successfully complete the courses, and of these more than 70 per cent get jobs within the industry.

WEB continues to provide first-class trades training for women who want to get straight on with a job in the industry. In addition, evening classes funded by CENTEC (Central London TEC) are now available for those who want to learn part-time.

WEB is a fully accredited NVQ and City and Guilds assessment centre that teaches NVQ Levels 1 and 2 in painting and decorating, plastering, bricklaying and carpentry and joinery, and City and Guilds in plumbing and electrical installation.

The benefits of a non-traditional career

At WEB we have found that women are extremely keen to pursue careers in the building trades. Indeed, around 70 per cent of our trainees go on to work in the industry. Others continue with full-time training.

Demand for our courses is so high that we currently have a two-year waiting list for most of them.

Many women are attracted to the building trades because they want to earn more than they could in traditionally 'female' occupations. Our trainees realise that by becoming qualified craftswomen they can gain financial independence, as well as have fulfilling careers.

3.2.3 Science and Technology Taster Course for Women

NORTH TYNESIDE COLLEGE

Staffing

This three-week course is staffed mainly by college lecturing staff, highly qualified in their respective areas. Some sessions are run by the trained staff from the Women into Work project based in North Shields. Most course sessions are based at the college, with field trips and industrial visits.

Target groups

All women, especially those contemplating returning to work, considering re-training, and those who never considered science when at school.

There are no entry requirements and no previous knowledge is assumed or required.

This is an 'open access' course. Potential students are counselled by the college Information Centre prior to the course so that they are aware of what is required and expected.

What is the course designed to do?

By the end of the course students will be aware of the variety of topics that are covered by science and technology, be able to relate these to women's experience and make an informed and considered judgement as to what further education and training they wish to undertake.

What is the course designed to lead on to?

Opportunities for future learning include GCSE, A-level, GNVQ intermediate and advanced in science, HEFC, Year 0 degree, basic electronics courses, basic IT courses, Access to Access: Science, nursery nursing. These qualifications are suitable for a range of careers in the chemical or pharmaceutical industries, the electronics industry, or for moving on to higher education.

Course content

We like to have the flexibility to vary aspects of the course after receiving feedback through the review and evaluation mechanism. Also we may make slight changes depending on the availability of staff and resources. The principles are unchanged and the general nature of the course remains studying science and electronics through practical and stimulating activities.

How is the course be organised?

Attendance is from 10.00 until 12.00, and then 1.00 until 3.00 pm, four days a week for three weeks. This gives a total contact time of 48 hours.

There is a short induction and enrolment period prior to starting the course proper.

An evaluation session takes place at the end of the course, involving all staff and students. The course is closely monitored by the Course Tutor and the Deputy Director, Curriculum, responsible for science courses.

All course records, including lesson evaluations, are collated by the Course Tutor.

Students may not wish to attend all sessions, although they will be encouraged to do so. They will be made aware at the start of the course that a minimum of 30 hours session attendance and achievement would be necessary to obtain a college certificate (or a TOCF certificate).

How are the students supported?

Counselling is provided prior to the course by the college Information Centre, Course Tutor and the Women into Work Project Leader. On-course advice includes careers advice. Follow-up advice will be offered by the college and Wallsend careers services.

A free crèche is provided. Help is available for women with particular difficulties, arranged by the North Tyneside Business Centre.

For the duration of the course, students have access to all college facilities, including the library, IT workshops, gymnasium, hair dressing salon, restaurant, etc.

The course is free.

How can women obtain credits for part-completion of the course?

If students do not complete 30 hours, they are invited to 'top up', either by attending this course at a later date, or by completing their hours via some of the other taster courses.

Assessment

Virtually all the sessions are practically-based or 'doing' activities. The students will therefore be assessed by their ability to complete the task. In electronics, for example, it will be the ability to complete the small electronics project, such as build an alarm. In chemistry, by being able to make your own cosmetic cream; in biology by being able to recognise various things under the microscope.

For non-practicals, such as careers advice, study skills, personal assessment will be used and recorded in a record of achievement.

All activities will be assessed by the tutor in charge of the session.

The concept of 'failure' is not part of the course philosophy and the lecturing staff will ensure that activities are designed with the course aims in mind. Assessment activities will be interesting, taxing but not stressful.

Evidence of learning

This will include the following:

- review and evaluation results
- samples of student work, such as the cosmetic cream or electronics project
- portfolio of evidence.

3.3 Enterprise, self-employment and professional development provision

The types of course in this Return to Work category represent trends that can be seen more widely in provision for women, even though there were few such submissions for this award.

For many women, particularly in rural areas and inner city locations, there may be few opportunities for paid employment. By identifying abilities they already have, developing business skills and gaining work experience, some women have managed either to set up their own businesses or have discovered how to utilise their talent in a variety of other ways. The three submissions in this category give a clear idea of how this kind of provision can benefit women.

3.3.1 Women Mean Business

DEVON COMMUNITY DEVELOPMENT AGENCY

Women Mean Business was set up under the ESF Community Initiative NOW (New Opportunities for Women). Its aim is to enable and encourage rurally-based women to become economically active, through self-employment, with an emphasis on co-operative working.

Enabling criteria

- women-only course
- held in local, community venues, not educational institutions, accessible by public transport
- women tutors
- held to fit in with school terms and times
- no course fees
- payment for cost of transport and childcare/dependant care
- no requirement for previous qualifications
- study skills help
- regular tutorials
- mentoring scheme to link students with people running businesses in their chosen fields
- advertised in local papers, radio, etc.

- open days held at supermarkets, community venues
- business support measures provided: clubs and businesses counselling available to graduate students, in course catchment areas.

Responsiveness and transferability

- situated in local venues, to enable access by rural women with limited transport
- course designed to acknowledge, validate and develop women's own experience
- flexible start and finish times to take account of childcare/dependant responsibilities
- nationally certificated course: BTEC Certificate of Business Administration
- course/qualification has been used by students in place of Access course, for entry to university and further training
- emphasis on confidence-building throughout, coupled with new-found skills, has enabled women to apply for and gain employment in a variety of fields
- assessment through practical assignments, involvement of outside agencies, e.g. banks, accountants, adult educational guidance
- development of *Good Practice* report on project for European Social Fund
- now working with WEA as sponsors to take advantage of European funding opportunities available.

Innovation and exploration

- involvement of wide range of interested agencies and funders, to meet recognised needs
- curriculum designed for this course
- emphasis on co-operative working
- franchised through Exeter College
- delivered on an outreach basis in rural areas
- regular, residential training for trainers sessions
- special project module designed to incorporate and reinforce learning in other modules, to provide students with feasibility study and business plan for own business, to launch them into self-employment

- project has linked with partners in Spain and Ireland. Now looking at developing, with them, aural materials, and supporting resources to enhance delivery in isolated rural areas
- transnational link has enabled sharing of resources and styles of delivery.

Evaluation

- use of Exeter College initial feedback and survey questionnaires to assess value and appropriateness of method, materials, style, resources, etc. Feeds back through team meetings, training for trainers, to change and develop course as appropriate
- *in camera* evaluation meetings of course groups, followed by evaluation by staff team and course representatives. Feeds back as above
- evaluation of accessibility and suitability undertaken by Sussex University student as part of third year thesis, in 1992. Feedback into 1993 course
- ongoing evaluation by Exeter University researcher, as part of PhD
- three-day transnational conference held in March 1994, to look at course progress, delivery, outcomes and future developments.

3.3.2 Women Only Business Course

ELEPHANT ENTERPRISES, LONDON

A 26-day course, run over 13 weeks, for women who are thinking of setting up in business for themselves. The course covers all aspects of setting up and running a business. Particular innovative points are:

- the subject is covered in far greater depth than the standard government/TEC-sponsored business short courses
- it has been designed specifically to meet the needs of women. Training methodology and materials have been specifically designed to include best practice in training women, including those from different ethnic cultures; female tutors are mostly used, guest speakers and role

models are women; tutors and guest speakers from a variety of ethnic backgrounds are used; sessions covering life planning, combining work with domestic responsibilities, skills evaluation, assertiveness and confidence-building, personal presentation and image, and personal safety are included

- recruitment and access procedures are designed to specifically encourage women, including ethnic minority groups and those with a disability, to apply. Priority for places is given to unemployed women and to obtaining a mix of different cultural backgrounds
- sessions are held at times convenient to women with domestic commitments. Trainees' childcare and travel costs are met and the programme is free of charge, including free lunch and refreshments
- training is supported by free individual counselling sessions run by an experienced woman business counsellor on an on-going basis for as long as required by the trainee, and by professional help in producing a business plan and raising business-start finance. Trainees are given free access to computing facilities for preparing their business plan and any other materials they require. Once the trainee starts her business, this support continues to be available free of charge
- all tutors are themselves experienced in running their own business
- much of the programme content is directly transferable to career planning, additional education or training or employment. At the end of the course, some trainees may decide they need further skills before starting their business, or find that the life-planning, skills analysis and confidence-building aspects enable them to go directly into employment, which is viewed as an equally positive outcome as going into business for oneself
- the programme is fully monitored at all stages. Trainees complete assessment forms for each session and for the programme overall. At the end of the course, Elephant Enterprises produces a full evaluation report. Recommendations for changes or improvements are transferred to both the subsequent course and to other courses run by Elephant Enterprises.

Innovative aspects

- tailor-made for women, particularly unemployed women and those from disadvantaged groups, and as well as using best practice methodology, covers a far wider range of subjects than do standard business start courses, thus providing trainees with a wider skills-base and wider range of options for their future
- designed and delivered by an organisation that specialises in business enterprise and provides comprehensive professional support services in this field, including help with raising finance
- includes access to free business and personal counselling and to computing facilities, with no time-limit for trainees to make use of these services.

Future developments

- setting up a business club/network for former and current trainees and other women in the area who are in business for themselves
- NVQ accreditation for Small Firms series of NVQs.

3.3.3 Enterprising Women Courses

WEA HIGHLANDS

These courses aim to meet the needs of women living in rural areas without access to local training opportunities. In 1993 courses were run in Skye, Nairn and Fort William; in 1994 courses were repeated in these locations but also provided in Brora, Aviemore and Tain.

The courses were run with support from:

- Highlands and Islands Enterprise
- Skye and Lochalsh Enterprise
- Lochaber Ltd
- Inverness and Nairn Enterprise
- ESF.

Those who took part in the course grew in confidence, discovered new interests and aptitudes. They identified new ways to apply existing skills and gained a variety of new skills that will be put to use in future training, voluntary or paid employment activities.

As organisers of the courses we are in no way complacent but always learning and attempting to find new ways to better meet the needs of the women involved.

From the course evaluation

For the past nine years the WEA has offered in the Highlands a range of pre-access courses, adult guidance SCOTVEC modules, health and personal development classes, as well as other learning opportunities. Initially our provision of women's education was concentrated in Inverness and Ross-shire but more recently new initiatives have developed in Lochaber, Skye, Caithness and Sutherland.

During the teaching of the adult guidance SCOTVEC module 'Options and Choices' it became apparent to the WEA that longer, more developed courses integrating guidance, computing and business skills, employment opportunities and work experience would meet an educational need, particularly in outlying areas not well served by a range of training opportunities.

The WEA decided to build on its community base and extend provision by developing the Women and Enterprise Opportunities course and offering a range of informal educational input with accredited SCOTVEC modules through Inverness College and other providers. After securing the support of Highland and Islands Enterprise and the three local LECs in the areas where training was to take place, an application to the ESF was made and in May1993 we heard that our project had been accepted.

Thirty-four women began 'Women and Enterprise Opportunities' and 30 completed the course, illustrating a high degree of commitment to training.

Aims

- to provide access for 30 unemployed women to a range of pre-vocational and vocational training opportunities on the theme of enterprise and work re-entry
- to offer relevant training and learning opportunities for women living in areas some distance from further education

- to offer an adult guidance and counselling service to trainees
- to minimise the traditional obstacles for women retraining and re-entering the labour market by offering payment towards transport and childcare costs
- to organise a comprehensive and accessible training programme by combining the community-based experience of the WEA with the resources of accredited providers such as Inverness College
- to boost confidence of the women taking part and increase their recognition of the skills they already possess.

What attracted women to the course

Most participants stated that computing first drew their attention, followed by free childcare and the fact that employment opportunities would be explored. Developing confidence, the building of new skills and a subsidy for travel were also reasons cited. Some women noted that the course fitted school times; others looked forward to the adult guidance component and help with CVs.

The structure of the course

Various training elements were organised before the course began, though the WEA wished to maintain as much flexibility as possible, to reflect more closely student interests and learning needs. A core WEA tutor led the Options and Choices section and offered support and teaching input throughout the remainder of the course. Fortnightly payments for travel and childcare were also organised by the core tutor.

Weeks one and two

- introductions and expectations of the course
- Options and Choices – Adult guidance SCOTVEC module
- identification of individual skills and interests
- exploration of transferability of domestic skills and voluntary experience
- investigation of possible training and employment opportunities with site visits and guest speakers
- development and evaluation of personal action plans.

Comments on the value of Options and Choices varied. Most of the women found it useful for assessing future plans and everyone seemed to enjoy and learn from the visits and speakers; many students felt their confidence increased. The women who studied the course over an intensive eight-day period in Skye felt energised and stimulated by the intensity of the personal development focus and felt that strong bonds developed between group members. Others who spent four weeks part-time on Options and Choices subject matter found it rather repetitive and too long. All agreed there was a need for clarity and close links with the rest of the course.

Weeks three and four

Introduction to computing. All three groups were offered accredited word processing modules. Almost everyone rated the computer training highly and would have enjoyed even more. Several students who had studied word processing in the past felt that the training could have been aimed at a more appropriate level. However, the WEA is committed to offering first step training and this must remain our priority for our target student group.

Weeks five to ten

This section of the course offered a range of possibilities depending on student interest and local cultural, social and economic differences. Students had a direct input into the direction each course took and often made suggestions for speakers and areas of study. In all three groups, three days were spent on book-keeping, business and marketing. The course also included a training day in Inverness and a number of site visits, guest speakers and personal development sessions.

The women appreciated being able to design to a great extent this section of the course to meet their needs. It was felt that the business and marketing sessions could be made more relevant to the needs of the women, perhaps by using a realistic case study of a small business. Additional input on the day-to-day running of a small business would also be welcome.

Almost everyone agreed that the guest speakers and site visits added an enriching element to the course and many women commented that they had learned new things about their own communities and established new contacts.

One of the most successful components of the course was the three-day work experience that all of the women undertook. Comments varied from 'brilliant', to 'very stimulating', to 'worthwhile'. Several of the women placed in a tourism-related activity, however, commented that it was 'very quiet', 'the wrong time of the year' or 'a waste of time'. The majority of those taking part felt that the work experience could have been longer – possibly lasting two weeks – and that in several instances more assistance could have been given to help organise suitable placements. Generally, though, the work experience was well received and, in several instances, may lead to employment.

Conclusions

All of the aims and objectives have been met. Those taking part grew in confidence, discovered new interests and aptitudes, identified new ways to apply existing skills and gained a variety of new skills that will be put to good use in future training, voluntary or paid employment activities.

The WEA has learned a great deal as well. We have found that offering non-accredited and accredited course inputs has allowed us to develop partnerships with other providers in these communities, thereby extending and co-ordinating the overall provision effectively.

3.4 Progression in work

Finally, in terms of provision for women that relates directly to their work there was one submisison only that referred to progression and advancement for women in work rather than for women returners.

3.4.1 Making Headway Programme

CAREERS RESEARCH AND ADVISORY CENTRE, CAMBRIDGE

Making Headway is a CRAC development programme for women managers in schools, colleges and universities. It is designed to help them progress to more senior positions within their organisations. It is a two-and-a-half day residential course, held twice since it was first piloted in December 1993.

The aims of the programme are:

- to enable women educationalists to identify strengths and skills gaps, and to develop action plans for personal and career goals
- to support women's development in education, encouraging the spread of good practice and the establishment of local/regional networks.

It is important and innovative because:

- it meets a need expressed by women in education for a programme designed especially for them
- it has been developed in partnership with public and private sector organisations (CambsTEC, Civil Service, Midland Bank). Other companies, e.g. Girobank, British Rail, have expressed interest in some form of involvement in 1995. This has enabled CRAC to offer the course at an affordable cost to participants who find commercial courses too expensive
- we are currently investigating other sources of funding, e.g. Fair Play Initiative, on the advice of Opportunity 2000
- the course itself offers crèche facilities, and is timed to be held in those periods of the year likely to be more accessible to women educationalists. One of the course

days is a Saturday, which participants have found helpful in their domestic arrangements
- feedback from the courses run so far is extremely positive.

Making Headway focuses strongly on helping women to 'break through the glass ceiling' and has the flexibility to be delivered nationally and locally and to be used by individuals.

Chapter 4

Return to Learn Provision

The four sub-groups in this chapter really merge into one, representing a wide range of provision for women who wish to return to learning for whatever reason. Many courses cater for a variety of learners, so that any division based on the main focus of the provision is misleading.

Return to Learn provision in a general sense has long been a first point of entry for women. As such it needs to be accessible and supportive of all those women who test out their ability in this way. The possibility of offering a range of progression routes and further options is a key component of many of these courses. In this the WEA and many FE colleges play an important role. The increasing use of the flexible OCN accreditation framework, at various levels and covering a whole range of provision, has not only opened up this route to many women, but, with recognised accreditation, qualified many courses for FEFC funding.

From the submissions in this category, it is clear that Return to Learn provision does not mean just study skills, even though the opportunity to rediscover or develop these is clearly important. Again, the flexibility of the OCN system allows for all kinds of learning experiences to be accredited at all levels, from entry level to Access to HE.

4.1.1 Introduction to Women's Studies

DONCASTER COLLEGE

Enabling criteria

Funding has been obtained to offer the course free, with free child-care support. The course is offered in three community locations during term-time only, for two hours per week. Premises that are regarded as non-threatening are used. Counselling on educational and/or personal matters is available from Doncaster College Counselling Unit.

Responsiveness and transferability

Feedback from students is built into the programme and responded to, e.g. the re-designing of a weekly learning diary sheet. The course design enables women to gain confidence and knowledge and to make choices on future action. The course has been accredited and is now a Schedule 2 course. Students have progressed to full-time and part-time courses or voluntary work and have increased in self-confidence and motivation.

Innovation and exploration

The course modules are:

- introductory module
- women in society
- women and media
- women and healthy living
- women taking control
- women and words
- women returning to work or study.

The course is accredited at SYOCF levels 2 and 3. Evidence is provided through a variety of sources, including advocate/tutor feedback. The course is designed to enable women to participate at different levels and to value each person's contribution and learning.

Staff have been involved in the development of the programme and attended the recognition and moderation panels. An evaluation and support session was also held.

Evaluation

The course design includes termly/modular evaluation from students and tutors. A termly meeting of tutors ensures that this feedback is responded to and appropriate changes made. It is hoped to further develop the course with additional modules.

4.1.2 WEA Margaret Sanders Branch

WEA THAMES AND SOLENT DISTRICT

This WEA women's branch was set up in memory of an Oxford woman. It aims to provide learning opportunities for women, in particular those who may find formal educational institutions daunting, or who may be excluded through poverty, lack of transport or childcare. Through its work, hundreds of women have been enabled to have the confidence to progress into further or higher education, employment and voluntary activity. Its Return to Learn courses are accredited through Oxfordshire Open College Network.

When the Branch started, its commitment to providing for women who were, for various reasons, excluded from mainstream adult education was unique in Oxfordshire. Its innovative approach, through outreach, community networking and responding flexibly to requests (and, indeed, raising the necessary funding) enabled the successful establishment of local learning groups for women that were free, with free crèches, held at times convenient to its users. This approach is now used extensively in similar provision throughout Oxfordshire, mostly funded through the LEA's Access budget.

The Margaret Sanders Branch encourages its students to become involved in the Branch's voluntary activities; students have become Branch Officers, and have made considerable contributions to publicity and fundraising; they have successfully campaigned for the maintenance of the Branch's funding. They also participate in decisions about future programmes.

The Branch is constantly innovative, looking for new ways to work with women. Recent examples include a self-advocacy group for women with learning disabilities, and collaborating with Oxford Black Women's Support Group. It tries out different forms of provision – from day schools, to residentials, to groups for users of Family Centres – as well as trying to develop new curriculum areas. It tries to expand women's expectations (e.g. in employment terms), to promote their understanding of the world they inhabit and to develop their confidence generally.

Guidance, individual support through tutorials and co-tutoring (where funding permits) are offered. The Branch has found that co-tutoring is immensely valuable as a form of staff development, as well as being a means of providing the necessary support to students. Paying part-time tutors to attend training events whenever possible has also been an effective way of developing the team. The Branch pays particular attention to appointing highly skilled and committed tutors on the principle that the provision is only as good as the tutors. It does its best to reward them appropriately.

Evaluation and monitoring is integral to all the Branch's work. This is achieved through constant feedback between tutors and students, formal gathering of statistical information, course diaries and tutors' written reports.

Programmes offered in various forms in the past two years include:

- New Opportunities for Women
- Speak Up for Yourself
- Looking at Women's Lives
- Assertiveness Training
- Booster Study Skills
- Writing Workshops
- Self Advocacy
- Return to Learn
- Learning for Earning
- Self Defence
- Brush Up on English
- Preparing for Maths GCSE
- Getting on with Maths.

4.1.3 Brush Up Your English and Maths

WEA EAST MIDLANDS

The programme started four years ago with outreach work being undertaken jointly by the WEA and Derbyshire County Council Community Education on a council estate in Matlock, Derbyshire. The target group was women, particularly those who were non-participants in adult education. A group of women were identified who met informally with pre-school children in the one facility on the estate, a one-roomed Terrapin building with one room on the edge of the moors. The group welcomed the outreach worker but were quite clear about not wanting any 'formal' education. The worker initially organised some keep-fit sessions, with a crèche worker running the crèche in one half of the room. Over a period of time the worker organised visits for the group, including the local FE college and adult education centre, and worked with the group to identify their needs. Every woman in the group was either a single parent or with an unemployed partner. All were living on state benefits. None had any minimum school leaving qualifications. Several were severely disadvantaged by low levels of literacy and numeracy and there was a recognition by the women that in order to get back into the labour market, which was a goal they all had, their lack of education was a negative factor.

The worker gradually introduced materials and by the end of the first year every woman was involved in working towards a C&G Wordpower and Numberpower qualification. Free crèche support backed up each session, taking place in the same room, with the group reluctant at first to separate from their children, despite the difficulties of trying to work with them around. It was clear that the continuing rationale for the group was coming together 'for the children' and justifying the space for themselves was hard. As the group got more involved in their work frustrations with the limited facilities grew; the worker suggested a move down to the adult education centre. Lack of confidence in going into a 'proper centre' was behind the group's resistance, but then fate took a hand in the form of the Terrapin's heating system, which died in the middle of the winter. The group moved down to the centre, a separate crèche was set up and the group 'took off' at this point.

The following year the class was opened up to others following discussions by the group, who chose the title 'Brush Up Your English and Maths' as non-threatening and informal. The group also wished the programme to remain women-only. This has been possible because life experiences personal to women (e.g. health issues) have always been used by the tutor as a vehicle for the work taking place. Similarly, the programme's overall aim is to help women back into the labour market after a period of full-time responsibility for childcare (Sex Discrimination Act 35 (1) (c) and 47).

Four years on the programme is now staffed by two tutors, one each funded by the WEA and the LEA. The course has continued to be offered for 36 weeks each year, in the daytime, in the adult education centre. It has continued to be free. A free crèche has supported the programme throughout its existence. The co-ordination for the programme has been provided by the WEA Tutor Organiser and the LEA ABE co-ordinator working closely together. Materials have been jointly provided by the two bodies. Accommodation has been provided by the WEA; extra facilities (e.g. access to computers) by the LEA.

Progression routes have been varied: they include an Access to HE programme, GCSE homestudy, university certificate course in social studies. One women from the original group is now working with the programme as a volunteer ABE tutor. All the other members of the original group have progressed to further education and training opportunities and employment locally.

There has also been a group progression. Six women from the original group progressed to the WEA 'Make Your Experience Count' course held in the centre. The experience of participating in these two programmes resulted in a request being made by these women to the WEA to form a WEA Women's Branch, which is currently being progressed.

The programme is reviewed by the tutors and co-ordinators at the end of each term, and learner evaluation, both oral and written, takes place mid-year and end of year. The programme is evaluated every year by the local WEA branch as part of its responsibilities. Feedback from learners has been taken on by the tutors and incorporated into the programme. The group still has a very strong cohesive identity, seeing itself as the 'Matlock Women's Group' and takes collective responsibility for the work of the programme and facilitating new members into the group. Socially, they mix outside the class and they have undertaken fundraising events to support the Centre, which has now become 'theirs'.

In summary we feel that this programme highlights the best practice in women's education:

- it has reached women who have been traditional non-participants in education through informal outreach work
- it is free provision with a free crèche, timetabled to suit women's domestic responsibilities

- it is located in a centre that is accessible, friendly and welcoming with café facilities providing lunch and snacks
- it has a very high level of worker support with two paid tutors, a volunteer tutor, an LEA ABE co-ordinator and WEA tutor organiser
- it provides ongoing educational guidance and counselling
- it has been innovative in adapting materials and teaching methodologies to the particular needs of learners and has always maintained a student-centred approach with negotiated learning
- it has been highly successful in enabling women to progress to further education, training, employment and community activism
- it has enabled women, through increased confidence and skills, to identify ways of working collectively to facilitate their own and other women's opportunities
- it has had the consistent commitment of the WEA and LEA, both prepared to prioritise and resource this work as a long-term development
- finally it sees a minor victory for cross agency-working in a climate that steadily pushes us into competition with each other rather than co-operation. It is important to recognise that the level of resourcing required by this kind of provision would not have been possible from either provider on its own. Only by joint resourcing and collaborative working practices has it been possible to increase opportunities for some women in Derbyshire.

4.1.4 Risca Outreach Project – Women's Return to Learn

RISCA, GWENT

A letter of recommendation from Glenys Kinnock MEP.

The Risca Outreach Project aims to enable women with young children to return to education and to provide a network of learning activities that allow for common group experience and individual progression. The target group is women with young children with mixed backgrounds, abilities, expectations and perceived needs, but with strong common ground.

The Project has evolved in a unique way. It started as a support group for women, then began to offer educational courses in response to the needs of the women attending the group. The Project is now 'two-pronged' in its approach. It runs a number of groups that provide courses for women on a wide variety of subjects such as DIY, Women's Health, Childcare, Psychology, Science, Welsh law, etc. while continuing to run a number of support groups for women around issues of concern to them.

The experience of the Project is that participation in these support groups encourages women to go on to educational courses. For example, the Project ran a domestic violence support group which, as well as looking at the emotional issues, also looked at the legal and other aspects of domestic violence. The skills developed by attending this group have enabled the women to progress to other courses.

To ensure that childcare responsibilities are not a barrier, the groups meet during school hours and a crèche is always provided. No fees are charged and the only costs incurred by women are minimal ones for tea and coffee, etc. This is particularly important in an area of high unemployment and poverty such as South Wales.

Since a lack of confidence often prevents women returning to education, the Risca Outreach Project ensures that the venues for the groups are accessible and have a friendly atmosphere. In recognition of the fact that the decision to return to education can be a very daunting step for women, the Project goes into women's communities to run its various groups in places that are familiar to the women, such as health centres, youth centres, etc. The Project also runs 'Taster' sessions that enable women to meet tutors and try out unfamiliar activities before committing themselves to a particular subject.

Another way in which the Risca Outreach Project removes potential barriers is by always having educational activities running on a 'drop-in' basis. This ensures that if all the groups are full when a women makes contact with the Project, there are still activities she can get involved with and she does not encounter a setback, having just taken the first step to return to education.

The groups run by the Project are firmly centred around the needs and interests of the women. Groups negotiate the overall curriculum and the content of each course, as well as the times and the conditions of study. New courses are continually developed in response to learners' needs and interests. Some groups that began as support groups for women have grown and developed according to the changing needs of the women involved.

Negotiating course contents and offering 'taster' days are an important and innovative way of providing guidance and learner support. In addition, there is an Outreach Worker who offers support to the women and, of course, the women in the groups offer unique support to one another.

Enabling the progression of women learners is a key factor in ensuring their continued participation. Besides enabling women to move on to new vocational opportunities or to courses in further and higher education when family circumstances permit, the Project offers courses for those women who are still reliant on childcare facilities. Most courses are accredited by the Open College Network, which means that these women do not miss out on a chance to gain qualifications or to further progress their education as a result of lack of childcare. The option of accredited courses in general enables women to gain qualifications in their own time and at their own pace.

The Risca Outreach Project believes that encouraging women to develop and pass on their particular skills and interests by becoming tutors themselves is an important aspect of empowering women learners and facilitating their educational progression. Continual skill-sharing is indeed a feature of the Project. Women learners have offered courses on topics ranging from Car Maintenance to Fine Arts and have taught locally and in other parts of the County of Gwent.

Women can and have built on the knowledge and skills acquired through some of the courses by going on to do more advanced courses in related subjects. For example, two groups that completed courses in Child Development Through Play went on to study Child Psychology, including experimental design and statistics.

A key element of the ethos of the Project is its responsiveness to the needs of women. The curriculum is another example of this. Many of its courses, such as childcare, are rooted in the women's everyday life experiences. This encourages the involvement of women and helps overcome such barriers as lack of confidence by introducing women to education in an area in which they have knowledge and feel relatively comfortable. The Project has found that these course then act as a 'launchpad' for their involvement in other courses. The Risca Outreach Project also encourages non-traditional roles for women by offering courses on subjects in which women are traditionally under-represented, such as maths, science and technology and DIY. The Project attempts to demystify these subjects by teaching them in a way that is fun and is also relevant to their lives. For example, the Project is currently running a course called 'RUBBISH', which looks at science from the perspective of what happens to our rubbish.

In many ways the proof of the success of the Project is the continued involvement and enthusiasm of its women learners, many of whom have achieved successes and who have become active in their communities. This year, because the school holidays meant that there would be no courses for six weeks, the women organised a summer playscheme. The women involved had all received training in work with under-fives, and after receiving extra training to work with older children they organised activities for up to 70 children, as well as workshops on a wide range of topics for the mothers. All the fundraising and the administration of the scheme was done by the women.

I have visited this project, which is in my constituency, and was enormously impressed by it, particular by the way that the women in the group are directly involved in decision-making. I talked to several women who had achieved great success and had acquired the confidence to pursue further educational goals. The atmosphere is friendly and co-operative and in my opinion represents very good practice.

4.2 Basic skills

There were several examples of provision designed specifically for those who need help with basic skills – mainly literacy and numeracy. Other provision recognises that some women may need such help and therefore provides this an an option. Several courses listed Wordpower and Numberpower as possible outcomes for their students.

4.2.1 Selby ALBSU Partnership

THE CYGNET CENTRE, SELBY

This scheme is a partnership between three agencies – Selby College, North Yorkshire Community Education Service and Selby Coalfield Industrial Chaplaincy. The course aims to provide life and social skills to young women who have had a disruption in their formal education for a variety of reasons. The course is an accredited course for City and Guilds Numberpower and Wordpower.

Background information

Selby Coalfield Industrial Chaplaincy supports workers and their families within local industries, i.e. Chaplains supporting people working in local mines, power stations, etc. One of the Chaplains is employed as a Youth and Community Chaplain whose brief is to work with local families. The Youth and Community Chaplain also works in partnership with the Community Education Service. As part of her duties, she is responsible for developing Daytime Projects. The project base is at the Cygnet Centre Selby. However, the work involved is to develop provision and opportunities for young women in the Selby district.

This has involved, over a period of time, the setting up of Women's Groups in Tadcaster, Barlby, Brotherton and three groups in Selby town centre. The groups were originally staffed by workers from the Community Education Service. However, the main aim of the groups is to enable the women to meet together to forge relationships in a supportive and caring environment, whilst encouraging them to undertake new and challenging issues in order for them to gain confidence and self-esteem. The workers involved in the groups encourage participation and engender empowerment, in order for the women to begin to run their own groups. A number of these women, through the encouragement of their peers and the workers, have gone on to further education. This has been on an *ad hoc* basis and now there is a perceived need to formalise this.

Three of the groups are currently supported fortnightly by Community Education Service staff and weekly by staff who run a supervised playroom for the children. This enables the mothers to have time for themselves.

The new project

The Youth and Community Chaplain has responsibility for supporting people in the community and developing group projects. The Women's Groups have given ready access to investigating the needs of young women in the Selby District. In order that work was not done in isolation, or duplicated, a meeting was arranged between the three partners.

From the evidence received from the Women's Groups, it became apparent that a specific need had been identified, which was basic skills for young women, who may have had a break in their formal education for a number of reasons: pregnancy, death in the family, illness, truancy, etc.

However, it was agreed that any provision that was set up would not be exclusively for these groups, although they would be encouraged to attend. The Community Education Service agreed to fund a worker for a short period to research into the need for this provision. The research findings have shown that there is a substantial number of young women who have had a disruption in their formal education and would benefit from such a project.

The three agencies – Selby Tertiary College, Selby Coalfield Industrial Chaplaincy and the Community Education Service – began to plan a way forward in order to address this issue whilst working in partnership.

Aim and objectives

- to provide basic skills in literacy and numeracy for young women who have had a disruption in their formal education and would benefit from such support

- to provide short courses for the target group from within the local community of Selby district, which will offer accredited learning (City & Guilds Numberpower and Wordpower) and which will enable participants to make informed choices about future progression.

Methodology

The project would be based in the local community, at the Cygnet Centre (Selby town centre), although should a need be identified elsewhere, alternative locations would be sought, particularly in view of the surrounding rural area. Contact would be made with people who would not normally involve themselves in education. The participants would be identified through established groups and through information and approaches to those young women identified through the research project.

Support

- the Community Education Service will provide Outreach Workers to recruit for the project
- Selby College will identify appropriate tutor(s) for the project, who will plan the detail of the programme and delivery to the groups
- Selby Coalfield Industrial Chaplaincy will identify appropriate crèche workers and provide premises
- it is intended that the management group would be made up of representatives from the existing partners, who will meet on a regular basis to manage the project
- a steering group will also be set up to include the existing partners from the management group, plus representatives from ALBSU, Health Service, Pupil Support Services, Careers. This group will meet three times a year throughout the life of the project.

Evaluation

A final report will be completed at the end of the project that will include tutors' evaluation and participant evaluation. The management group will undertake monitoring of the project to ensure that the curriculum is responding to the needs of the participants.

Performance indicators

These will be determined by:

- the numbers who start the course
- the numbers who complete the course
- those who are accredited with City & Guilds Numberpower and Wordpower
- numbers progressing to further education.

Dissemination

The representatives from the management group will promote the project within their own organisations and on a county-wide basis through the Community Education Service and to other local organisations and voluntary groups. The report of the project will be made available to any other interested parties.

4.2.2 Return to Study Skills for Women

GORSEINON COLLEGE

Purpose and objectives

The purpose of this programme is to enhance both personal competence and confidence in women who have suffered exclusion from the labour market because they lack basic skills. It aims to develop those personal, social and study skills necessary for the beneficiaries to cope with a return to the labour force or to a period of higher level training.

The primary objective of the programme is to enable the beneficiaries to achieve national accreditation in Return to Study via the National Open College Network at Entry Level.

Evidence that has been collated and assessed at the College over the past four years indicates the need for such provision. Currently, some 75 per cent of students on 'First Step' study programmes at the College are women, of whom some 60 per cent have no recent experience of paid employment and who cite a lack of confidence and a lack of guidance and information as real barriers that prohibit a smooth return to the labour force. Such evidence has been substantiated by monitoring enquiries at the College and our Open Learning Centre.

The College works in close partnership with the Employment Service, Chwarae Teg, and the West Wales TEC and holds the local contracts for delivering both Jobclub and Jobplan, and Training for Work. This enables the College's Management Teams of the Adult and Community Education and Business Centre programmes to liaise constantly with local employers and understand local labour market trends and to be aware of the training needs of a local pool of unemployed people.

Recruitment

Taster sessions are organised periodically at the College in addition to sessions at outreach events such as the Valley Women's Roadshow. Visits by staff and distribution of marketing leaflets are organised with Job Centres, Jobplan Workshops, Restart Courses, local libraries, health centres, playgroups and community centres, and a drop-in facility for advice and guidance is available at our Open Learning Centre.

Guidance

Each beneficiary receives an individual guidance/advisory interview. On-course guidance and support forms a major part of the programme, in addition to induction and exit training. The on-course guidance incorporates job search, assessing local employment trends, compiling CVs, computer aided guidance programmes, action planning, guest speakers and progression routes to further education and training.

Course structure

The course structure allows flexibility to respond to individual needs, including the needs of students with special needs and physical disabilities.

Cost/fees

There are no course fees and students are provided with all necessary resources, including files for portfolio submission.

Care costs/travelling expenses

Students who have young children or other dependants who need care, receive help with these costs, together with help towards travelling expenses.

Course times/dates

Courses start at various times during the year and the structure of the course allows each participant who is claiming benefits to remain in search of, and available for, employment throughout.

All courses are arranged within school hours and terms, to assist women with domestic commitments.

Staff development

All staff delivering the programme are qualified and experienced in working with adults. Staff development is continuous and staff regularly attend seminars involving the needs of women and are actively involved with local networks such as West Glamorgan Women's Initiative Group, Valley Women's Roadshow Committee, together with the Chwarae Teg Project.

Monitoring, reviewing and evaluation

Monitoring and reviewing of the programme and students needs is a continuous process and adaptations are implemented according to needs. All students progress to employment or further education or training courses, with the majority progressing to Access to Further Education courses.

Students complete evaluation forms at the end of the course, and a further evaluation form three to six months following completion of the course.

4.3 Access

A range of needs is also recognised in some of the Access provision. Even though this group includes those courses that lead to a validated Access qualification and are recognised as a route into higher education, there were also alternative progression routes for those women who needed them. In addition to a certificate of entry to HE or sufficient OCN credits, the flexibility of the system allows for alternative certification and progression.

4.3.1 Fresh Start Women's Access Course

THE SHEFFIELD COLLEGE

Fresh Start is an Access course specifically designed for women for whom a return to mainstream education is an appealing but daunting prospect. The course runs over two years, the student attending one day each week. It is accredited through SYOCF. It is possible for the women to attend the course and to contribute through discussions and work carried out during the course days. It is also possible for women to carry out written work which, if assessed to be at a higher level as idcntified by SYOCF criteria, would enable them to gain sufficient credits to be awarded a certificate of entry to higher education. Thus the course successfully manages to accommodate a broad range of academic ability and needs.

The course is designed to give students a thorough grounding in social and political studies through a combination of local, national, international and global perspectives. The central focus over the two years is the concept of *Inequalities* and an examination of the distribution of resources and opportunities in Britain and worldwide. The course is carefully designed to enable women to progress in confidence in examining issues. From an initial examination of their own and their families' experience, they are encouraged to move on to consider the wider experience of people other than themselves.

In curriculum terms the course is innovative in taking a multidisciplinary approach, combining the areas of social and political studies and development studies. The subject areas of Literature, Geography, History and Sociology are used as tools of analysis that together offer insight within our general themes. In this way, knowledge is demystified, confidence is developed and the student comes to realise that self-motivation is the key to learning.

The target groups in recruiting for this course are working-class women; women who have felt themselves to have been failed by the education system; black women; disabled women. The course has been running successfully since 1989, and recruitment occurs by word of mouth initially. However, each year the tutors publicise the course details through local community organisations. Local press and radio are used to specifically encourage target groups to apply. Each applicant is interviewed by one of the tutors to make sure that the nature of the course is fully understood and that the course is suitable for the applicant.

Fresh Start is held in a local neighbourhood centre whose primary purpose is to provide informal learning opportunities for adults in the community. This, together with the informal setting of soft chairs, sofas, carpets and a general 'non-college' atmosphere, is an important element that the staff maintain in order to allow for a supportive and non-threatening environment. A crèche is provided in the same building. The course runs during the day to enable women to attend to their children at school.

A wide range of 'special needs' and specific difficulties regarding literacy have been presented by students on this course. The tutors have been involved in accommodating these needs as a matter of priority. For example, tutorials have been carried out in the homes of wheelchair users; special arrangements have been negotiated with the university libraries to allow disabled students to receive borrowers' rights. Students with eye disorders have had specially enlarged hand-outs to enable them to have a better chance of comprehending course materials. However, most work in the area of basic literacy skills development has been carried out in one-to-one tutorial sessions – an integral part of the course.

Specific skills that are 'transferable' to other learning situations are practised on the course. A wide range of research skills including interviewing, designing surveys and questionnaires, using cataloguing systems and basic use of information technology are introduced during the first year of the course. In the second year, students are given the opportunity to present work in the form of a seminar. Time-constrained essay practice is also part of the second year.

Students have progressed successfully to HE courses at Sheffield University and Sheffield Hallam University. Most of these students have been surprised and delighted in what they have been able to achieve. Only very few have a clear HE target at the outset. Most have taken the two-year access course to discover this for themselves. Our first graduates were awarded their university degrees in 1994 from the first intake in 1989. They have gained Social Studies and BEd degrees. Currently, Fresh Start students are taking undergraduate courses in Women's Studies, Applied Social Studies, Communication Studies, Law, Archaeology and Pre-History, Occupational Therapy and Building Science.

4.3.2 Access Programme (Women-Only Routes)

HUDDERSFIELD TECHNICAL COLLEGE

Access to HE programmes

Access aims to prepare mature students for higher education by encouraging them to develop the necessary skills and confidence to perform effectively at degree or diploma level. It is part of a national movement that aims to promote equality of opportunity. Access to HE students need no previous qualifications in order to embark on Access work. To facilitate this, two principles underpin its methodology:

- the curriculum develops from and reflects the experience and knowledge of the students
- the learning strategies are investigative and student-centred, emphasising skills rather than knowledge: hence the emphasis for all students on study skills, research techniques and group interaction.

It is cross-college and modular, featuring vocational routes in social science, arts, science, computing, business and leisure studies, art and design and business studies with language.

In order to avoid the difficulties associated with modular provision (loss of coherence, lack of student motivation, high dropout) the programme has a common core and each student is allocated a tutor who teaches substantially on Access and who is responsible for ensuring the student makes progress. The course is designed on a credit accumulation basis and works on the principle of modules. Students have to complete seven modules over a period of time that suits them, two examinations and one final assignment in their 'final' year of study to gain their certificate. There is therefore almost complete flexibility in the programme design.

Access is delivered at the main site, with some modules (computing, sociology, maths, literature and study skills) being delivered on an outreach basis. We target outreach centres that recruit both working-class women and women from ethnic minority backgrounds.

We have since 1986 run New Opportunities for Women courses in partnership with Leeds University on an outreach basis. We therefore offer Women's Access Modules on the same basis as NOW provision at outreach centres, 9.30 am–3.00 pm, crèche provision, no fees, tutorial support. We are also developing packages for flexible delivery and open learning and investigating the possibility of accrediting women's experience in the home/part-time work against Access modules.The course is validated by NEAB, UKCC and WNYAN.

Currently our provision is designed to enable women to complete their Access Programme within one year by taking their childcare, financial and personal situation into account. There is a sessional crèche, and a nursery; we pay crèche, nursery and childcare costs where needed; we run school children's activity weeks when school terms differ from those of the college; we provide toys and equipment, etc. for children if mothers need to bring them into the classroom; we have 60 Training for Work places where we prioritise single parents (mostly women), particularly for childcare costs, but also for the extra £10 weekly and travel costs.

Women on most benefits pay no fees. Women dependent upon husbands can get a minor award to pay their fees and each woman is assigned a personal tutor to help guide and support her academic programme and to deal with any personal matters that come up. We regularly deal with domestic violence, child custody cases, homelessness and issues arising from poverty generally.

We have, however, designed Access to be flexible enough to cope with these emergencies, so even if a women has to 'drop out' for a period of time the credits she has gained whilst on the course remain hers and she can return at the point of leaving, not at the beginning.

Our philosophy on the Women's Access Courses is similar academically to that outlined for the general Access Programme. However, apart from this and the practical support we offer women, we do aim as committed feminists to integrate a gender perspective into the academic disciplines they study. We hope to empower women by introducing them to a way of interpreting the society in which they live that enables them to understand their place as women in a patriarchal culture. We also aim, by facilitating their progress to higher education, to help them towards financial independence for themselves and their children should they choose to be or remain independent.

Many women who were our students are now working as teachers, social workers, youth and community workers, etc. From Access women have gone into medicine, physiotherapy, social work, teaching, community work, podiatry, arts, science, humanities and social sciences degrees – this year we have a woman who wants to go on to architecture.

We have a standard course review and evaluation procedure as part of our quality audit. As a result of this review, we organised a week-long residential for women and children called Preparing for Higher Education, in partnership with Kirklees Metropolitan Council and Northern College.

Last year 120 students completed their certificates and most went on to higher education. Of these 120, 75 were women and of the 75, 42 were doing Women-Only Access Modules. Of these 42, 15 were from ethnic minority backgrounds and two had special needs. Forty women had offers from higher education institutions.

4.3.3 Certificate for Mature Students – Women's Route

DEPARTMENT OF GENERAL EDUCATION, BRADFORD AND ILKLEY COMMUNITY COLLEGE

Background

The Certificate for Mature Students (CMS) has been running at Bradford and Ilkley Community College for 10 years. Over the past few years a combination of MA research by a staff member around the needs of women returners, on-course research looking specifically at the needs of women on the CMS and the impact of the recession on the gender balance of the course convinced the course team that a women's route was needed.

Women students on the course said that two priorities for them were childcare and study time built into the course. They found it very difficult to study at home because of domestic demands.

Development of the course

Existing research has shown the value of women-only provision and all-women tutor teams. It was decided that the physical base would be a local upper school, committed to working with adults and with a good crèche.

The school, Carlton Bolling College, was very supportive of the plan and allocated a base room and nursery places to the students, as well as a small office for the teaching team.

The course was timetabled – as are all CMS courses – between 9.30 am and 3.00 pm. It ran for three days per week, and the curriculum incorporated directed study, a new Women in Society module and Literature (history was studied on the other courses).

The course followed the CMS format of termly course committees run by the students.

Experience of delivery

The course recruited 18 women, local to the area. Fourteen were single parents. One woman transferred to another course and one had a premature baby but is returning to the course. All the others passed the first year very successfully – the only CMS group to achieve this. One completed the two-year course in one year and entered teacher training.

The women-only format proved extremely supportive, but also threw up difficult and painful issues. It was the feeling of the course team that women who might not have succeeded in other groups achieved their full potential.

The directed study slot was crucial to the success of the course. Women were highly motivated and worked very hard. The solid grounding in the first year meant that the second year could run for two days per week quite satisfactorily.

All students passed CLAIT 1 and several passed CLAIT 2 with distinction, although they had initially been resistant to studying IT.

The future

The Women in Society module has been offered across CMS and proved very popular with staff and students.

The Carlton Bolling Women's Route model has been offered at another centre – Bradford Training and Information Centre – and has recruited well. Again, the centre has a good crèche and is an enthusiastic partner.

The model has been adapted as a result of feedback from students and course committees. Changes include building in extra time for GCSE English and splitting the GCSE maths slot. The success of the course, which is aimed at working-class women, is based on partnership, crèche provision, appropriate curriculum and a very high level of support.

4.3.4 Access for Women into Art

KENT ADULT EDUCATION

Women who want to enter college to study Art and Design can now take advantage of a course that will help them build a portfolio of work suitable for entry to Higher Education. The course, Access for Women into Art (AFWIA), is validated by Kent Access Consortium and registered with the Higher Education Quality Council as one of the new Access to Art and Design courses available in Kent.

Access to Art courses are offered by colleges of further and higher education, but Access for Women into Art is the first one in Kent to be based in an adult education centre. This offers a number of advantages both in programme content and in delivery.

In adult education we are familiar with the needs of students with family responsibilities and take these into account when planning courses. Gillingham Adult Education Centre has a crèche that takes children from six weeks, for which students pay preferential rates. Our programme also takes account of local school times, finishing at 3.00 pm and breaking during half-term and school holidays. These special considerations can make it easier for women with childcare responsibilities to pick up and develop their study in Art and Design. Gillingham Adult Education centre is situated in the town centre, close to all amenities, including fast rail links to London and the Kent Coast, which is an advantage for students travelling from outside the Medway Towns.

AFWIA philosophy

Access for Women into Art (AFWIA) offers students an opportunity to study in a supportive environment while addressing issues that are relevant to managing work and home commitments alongside ambitions as artists. A wide variety of materials and approaches are used: sculpture; painting; design; photography; drawing; printmaking and written work.

The AFWIA programmes seek to provide positive role-models of women as artists, and contain a theoretical element that focuses on the relationships of gender, class, age and 'race' in cultural production and consumption. Examples of good practice are shown in slide shows, talks, visits by women artists and designers, visits to exhibitions and through discussions that place studio work within its historical context. The work of women artists and 'artists of colour' is shown in balance with examples of mainstream Western Art practice.

The 1994/5 Access for Women into Art programme has received support from The Laura Ashley Foundation for study trips and specialist lecturers.

The programmes of study

AFWIA offers three paths of study – a certificated programme, a pre-certificate programme and an advanced programme. The certificated programme, AFWIA Certificate, is designed as a multi-exit course, providing routes to a variety of art and design studies. Candidates who successfully complete the course receive a certificate validated by Kent Access Consortium, whose membership is drawn from colleges such as Mid-Kent College, Kent Institute of Art and Design and Christ Church College. The certificate should also be recognised by colleges outside the county who are running similar degree and diploma level art and design courses. Students are guaranteed an interview at colleges represented by the Consortium. Contact is maintained with the Kent colleges to which students may progress. Past students have taken up part-time and full-time study in Fine Art, Ceramics, Display, Graphics, Foundation Studies, Art and Sociology, and Teacher Training. Most students may have the ultimate intention of progressing to college but the course is also suitable for women who wish only to increase their knowledge and understanding of the creative process. The pace and content is challenging and broad. The pre-AFWIA course is a new course that is aimed at providing a grounding in basic skills for those who are preparing to move into the certificated programme. Many of the art and design practices in the certificated course will be covered in the pre-AFWIA course, but at an introductory level. AFWIA Advanced is intended for those who have been through advanced programmes of study and wish to continue to work on the development of professional studio practices. The precise content of this course is developed in consultation with group members and is intended to provide a greater focus on sustained projects that relate to more advanced learning.

4.4 Recognising cultural difference

Flexibility in the provision is also important for those women for whom English is not their first or only language. Whilst some courses have a specific ESOL input, others recognise that this may be needed for some of the women who enrol and therefore make such provision. Although there were only three specific courses where language support was the primary intention, there were many where the needs of women from various ethnic minority backgrounds are recognised and met.

4.4.1 Openings for Women

BRADFORD LANGUAGE SCHOOL, BRADFORD AND ILKLEY COMMUNITY COLLEGE

The course is designed for women from a wide variety of countries and social and educational backgrounds who, for cultural or personal reasons, prefer women-only classes.

Its aims are threefold:

- to develop the students' written and spoken English in order to enable them to function effectively in the UK
- to develop their personal confidence so that they will be able to act independently
- to develop an appreciation and knowledge of their role in contemporary society and to enable them to make informed choices and decisions on behalf of themselves and their families.

The course requires a high level of commitment from the students and a regular attendance for nine hours per week, 36 weeks per year. All students are counselled before, during and after the course.

It is innovative in ethos, time allocation, variety of levels and curriculum. Within five levels students can progress at their own speed, having time to develop according to individual need. Students are not restricted to one level at any one time, but can choose additional options across levels; for example cursive writing, magazine production, drama, spelling.

The curriculum starts with a practical framework of language for coping in English, and then develops into a framework of ideas, until, in the newly formed modular course, the language development is tailored to the subject requirements.

Additional literacy support is provided; keyboard skills and conversation classes are also available.

The most recent innovation has been Living and Working in Bradford, a course designed to follow level five and developed this year in response to student demand. It is designed specifically to meet the needs and widen the horizons of linguistic minority women in Bradford.

4.4.2 Outreach Programme – Bilingual Work with Asian Women

DEPARTMENT OF CONTINUING EDUCATION, LANCASTER UNIVERSITY

Aims

To develop and encourage bilingual learning and progression opportunities amongst Asian women who are not able to participate in mainstream education because of:

- lack of fluency in English
- childcare needs
- lack of transport
- family commitments that inhibit regular attendance
- a need for single sex provision
- a need for accessibility and timing to accommodate domestic needs.

Nature of the scheme

The scheme offers a variety of bilingual short courses and topics to complement and work with college or community provided English classes. The courses are delivered by bilingual, Asian, female tutors who use their bilingual skills to:

- encourage critical thought and discussion at a level that reflects the women's intellectual ability, rather than fluency in English
- reinforce concepts presented in English that can be followed up during the week in English classes

- build confidence and self-esteem
- widen the range of topics available to women attending community classes
- provide opportunities for accreditation of skills other than English through Open College, pre-GCSE, Foundation scheme
- monitor and research participants' perceptions of education, university education and preferred teaching methods, through interviews in the mother tongue.

Course topics include: assertiveness training; career awareness and interview skills; welfare rights; health and education issues.

The courses are currently in two locations:

- Preston, working in collaboration with a community centre, managed by the Gujarat Hindu Society
- Brierfield (East Lancs), working in collaboration with Nelson College, who provide English classes in Brierfield community centre.

The innovative element

- a genuine partnership between college, university and community centre
- a negotiated curriculum in consultation with local community contacts and tutors
- an opportunity for Asian women to experience a variety of teaching and learning styles such as role play, group discussion, etc.
- a mutual opportunity to raise awareness – of university study options for the women; and inform the university of the needs of Asian women
- an opportunity to build on the women's bilingual skills and existing educational background, rather than implement a learning programme that emphasises only English language skills
- an opportunity for some women to consider employment options.

Evaluation

A number of women have widened their perceptions of personal opportunities and the nature of university study in England. Many women have been able to demonstrate their actual learning ability as well as improve their language fluency.

There is evidence that the more intensive, mother-tongue, interview evaluation method is increasing motivation and self-esteem, as well as providing valuable cultural information relating to learning needs. It is hoped that final outcomes of the research process will inform the university and other providers of the ever-changing cultural implications affecting study in Britain for Asian women arriving in Britain during the 1990s.

Chapter 5

Return to Re-assess Provision

5.1 Re-orientation and re-entry courses

This category is a collection of a variety of kinds of provision, all of which offer a wide range of opportunities to women. It includes some well-tried and evaluated types of reorientation courses that allow women returners to explore a whole range of options for their future in a supportive group. It also includes some new kinds of provision that have been developed in response to emerging needs.

Some of the earliest educational provision designed specifically for women that developed during the 1970s was modelled on New Opportunities for Women (NOW) courses. Although the meaning of this title has changed in the light of recent EC initiatives, the essential component of a course that provided women with a chance to discover, in a supportive group, what their interests and potential might be, remains an important part of the overall provision for women. Despite the emphasis on vocational input and the need for accreditation, it was heartening to find that a number of the submissions retained the key elements of this kind of provision. Both FE colleges and the WEA – which pioneered many such courses – made submissions whose descriptions showed that the key characteristics of good practice remain. Whilst some made no mention of formal accreditation, others showed how OCN credits had enhanced their provision and provided recognition of their courses.

5.1.1 Awaaz Women's Training Project

SHEFFIELD

Aims

Awaaz is a voluntary organisation run by Asian women for Asian women. We are committed to the advancement and empowerment of Asian women through providing recognised training and education.

Awaaz offers a unique and innovative training programme that adheres to the following principles:

- all Asian women have skills; we value those skills and build on them
- we acknowledge the different experiences women bring and base the course on sharing and negotiation
- we provide a safe, confidential training environment.

Awaaz runs a one-year training programme offering computer and study skills, confidence-building, awareness-raising and project-based study that is accredited up to Level 3 by the SYOCF. The training is delivered in a supportive and appropriate environment by Asian women trainers at an Asian women's centre.

Recruitment

The Awaaz Asian women in Britain course is open to Asian women who are long-term unemployed and for whom other forms of education and training may be inaccessible. All Asian women are welcome and student groups have included women of Indian, Pakistani, Bangladeshi, Sri Lankan and Chinese origin.

Recruitment activities are particularly aimed at women who are isolated in the community such as single parents, women who have experienced violence and abuse within the family and women who, because of resistance to their personal development within family or community, need a safe and confidential learning environment. To access information and training, women in this target group have to overcome personal fears and lack of confidence; lack of confidence in using English; the pressure of domestic commitments; and inappropriate and discriminatory provision in many institutions.

Student support

The course is free and the hours enable women on benefits to continue to claim. Student learning is supported by travel allowances to cover all bus fares, crèche provision or payment for childcare according to individual need, and the provision of stationery and learning materials. Classes take place within school hours and during school terms only.

The course incorporates strict guidelines to ensure confidentiality and mutual respect for all students, aiming to create a safe environment in which students can share frankly their thoughts and experiences as Asian women in Britain on the issues that are most important to them.

Course content

The 'Asian Women in Britain' course is taught in three modules, and students can join and leave at the beginning of each module, receiving credits for the modules they have completed. Each stage involves discussion and negotiation with the students and is adapted to meet their needs.

Module I

This element includes: confidence building and assertiveness activities; looking at black history through colonialism, the history of black communities in Britain and the place of Asian women in building that history; looking at issues of oppression and violence and how they affect us as Asian women.

Module II

Asian women workers in different agencies and professions are invited to speak about the service their agencies provide and their own roles. The speaker inputs provide role models of Asian women in employment and stimulate critical discussion of the extent to which Asian women are provided or denied key services they are entitled to.

Issues covered include the impact of matrimonial and immigration law; housing issues and health care; violence and abuse; access to education and employment; and other issues affecting Asian women.

Module III

This module involves placement experiences in a statutory or voluntary organisation offering services to black communities, and a long project done individually or in groups, which can be based on some aspect of the placement experience or be entirely separate.

Alongside these modules we also offer weekly sessions in 'English and Study skills' and 'Computing Skills', taught by the same tutors but held in The Sheffield College, rather than at the Asian Women's Centre. The purpose of these sessions is to support and consolidate the learning experienced on the main course and to introduce students to the college environment with the support of tutors they trust. Students can also join other classes on the main college site alongside the Awaaz course.

Progress beyond the course

The project expects that all trainees will leave with a minimum of nine and a maximum of 18 credits from levels 1 to 3 of the SYOCF. These can be added to other credits accumulated and used to gain entry to further and higher education.

Awaaz offers a safe and supported introduction to the college environment for women who originally did not feel able to attend classes at a local neighbourhood centre. The confidence-building elements that run through the curriculum are designed to empower women to hold their own both on their placement experience and in any work or training environment they choose to move on to.

The skills and confidence gained will enable trainees to engage in a wide range of voluntary activities in the community, to share their skills and understanding, to support other women in developing their potential and to raise awareness in formal and informal ways.

Their achievements on the Awaaz course will enable a smaller proportion of women to move directly into employment (or self-employment) such as translating and interpreting work, jobs in voluntary sector women's organisations, or in statutory agencies where knowledge of Asian communities and fluency in an Asian language are specifically requested.

In areas such as health care and education, social and community care, advice work and advocacy services, there is a severe shortage of black women workers who can offer a combination of fluency in a community language, a theoretical understanding of the role of welfare agencies and principles of confidentiality and non-directive counselling, and the professional skills to provide advice, support and education in their own communities.

Monitoring

The course incorporates continuous feedback and discussion with students to monitor what they are getting out of it and what changes need to be made. Students are also asked for written feedback at the mid-point and end of each module and are asked to assess their own progress. Individual tutorials and guidance sessions allow detailed monitoring of each student's progress and experience of course content.

As the course is flexible according to the needs of each student group, the tutors evaluate and revise materials and delivery at the end of each module. The course is also moderated and evaluated by the moderator from the SYOCF through regular visits and final moderation.

In conclusion, the Awaaz 'Asian Women in Britain' training course offers a powerful, often life-changing learning experience for women who have been severely disadvantaged in the fields of education and training. The course provides a uniquely intense opportunity to learn new skills, develop confidence and explore important social issues that are also deeply personal and difficult to discuss in most other forums that Asian women have access to. We believe the course is a model of good practice in its insistence on a safe environment free from oppressive behaviour and a curriculum appropriate to the life experiences of the women on the course.

5.1.2 New Start for Women

WILLIAM NEWTON FE CENTRE, STOCKTON-ON-TEES

Aims

- to provide a bridge into training, further and higher education and employment for women who have been out of paid work or have been limited to low paid, unskilled part-time work for a considerable time because of family responsibilities

- to provide guidance and information on new directions to women who need to retrain because of redundancy or disability
- to provide a supportive and stimulating environment with affordable childcare to women currently engaged in bringing up young children, helping them cope effectively and enabling them to prepare for their next step
- to enable women to develop basic transferable IT skills, their written and oral communication skills and their ability to work successfully with others
- to enable women to develop confidence in themselves and recognise their abilities through the study of a range of subjects in a supportive atmosphere.

Nature of the scheme

New Start is a one-day a week course for women that runs for 24 weeks in school terms and school hours and has its own crèche. Students take taster courses in Social Studies, English and Information Technology. These are built around weekly opportunities sessions that aim to:

- create awareness of strengths via confidence-building and assertiveness
- help women identify opportunities in training, further and higher education in the local area that match their abilities, personal qualities, interests and potential
- give guidance and support with preparation of CVs and interview skills.

Each student follows a 24-week morning course in Social Studies and Opportunities, a 12-week afternoon course in Information technology and a 12-week course in English and Further Opportunities.

Individual counselling tutorials are timetabled for an hour every week for each group. In these, students can discuss study problems, personal matters affecting their studies or seek individual careers guidance.

The course is taught by four women tutors, one of whom has the role of Course Organiser. All are graduates, three are trained teachers and one is a trained and experienced counsellor currently following a teacher training course. The course team share a large amount of experience in adult, especially women's, education. The Course Organiser and two of the tutors are part-time adult education tutors. One tutor is employed full-time by Stockton Sixth Form College.

The course is based at the William Newton Further Education Centre, a local authority adult education centre with 5000 part-time students. The course crèche is at the Centre, which also houses a pre-school playgroup and a school nursery.

Stockton Sixth Form College provides the tutor and first-class facilities for the IT component of the course at their site, which is a five-minute journey from the William Newton FE Centre. Transport by minibus is provided for New Start students between sites.

The Course Organiser works with and is responsible to the management at Stockton Sixth Form College and the Principal of the William Newton FE Centre. Both managements have given their full support to the New Start initiative and have actively collaborated in its development. In 1994–95, following the first two successful years of New Start, Stockton Sixth Form College has become the chief funder via the FEFC and students are now registered as students of the sixth form college.

All course publicity makes clear that all ages are welcome, no qualifications are required and that disabled students are welcome.

Students with special needs

A training event for adult education tutors in Cleveland on the needs of disabled students in further education took place in May 1994 in response to a request for staff training on this issue by a New Start tutor with disabled students in her group.

As a result of this training event and the input to it from disabled students and tutors, including New Start students, positive action has been taken by the Cleveland Adult Education Service to make clear in the 1994/95 prospectuses that disabled students are welcome on courses and to highlight the facilities available at individual centres for disabled students.

The New Start prospectus entry was also amended:

- to make clear that disabled students were welcome on the course
- to encourage prospective students with a disability to inform us in advance if they wished to so that their special

needs could be discussed and appropriate support organised in advance.

We also learned the importance of helping disabled students to integrate with the rest of the group and were helped to think about how this could be achieved. Appropriate action was taken.

Innovation and good practice

We identified the importance of IT skills to women's employment prospects; more than 50 per cent of female employees now use computers at work. There was concern that the number of women entering computing and information technology as a career was going down rather than rising, and these considerations led to the following developments:

- an Introduction to Computing module in the course
- development with Stockton Sixth Form College of a progression route from this to an RSA CLAIT I certificate course
- provision of information on further routes of progression, e.g. NVQ Level 2 in Business Administration at Stockton and Billingham Technical College, Women into Financial Maths and Information Technology Diploma course at the University of Teesside – a free part-time women's access course.

The importance of transferable skills was also recognised through:

- helping women to recognise the transferable skills that they possess but often do not realise they possess
- helping women to develop transferable skills in:
  - IT
  - written and oral communication
  - working with others
- recognising the value of having evidence of these skills to present to prospective employers and introducing National Record of Achievement folders validated by the NEAB, Teesside TEC and Cleveland County Council.

Guidance and support were essential ingredients:

- the experience of tutors over a number of years has generated an awareness of the many problems women face

that can prevent them from being effective students. The introduction of a tutorial system into the course has been effective in helping students deal with these problems in the early stages of the course and enabled us to offer time for discussion of future directions on an individual basis
- the provision of support with basic English and maths through co-operation with the Adult Basic Education Co-ordinator.

Conclusion

We recognise that different women have different needs. Some women may need to be breadwinners in full-time employment, some may be seeking satisfaction and fulfilment in more skilled or better paid part-time work or wish to make a commitment to voluntary work, others may be seeking self-development or new interests through further or higher education. It is important to the success of the course each year that women are asked whether the course matches their needs and expectations and to use regular feedback to negotiate and develop the curriculum and its delivery.

5.1.3 Women, Work, Skills

WEA LEICESTER

Aims and nature of scheme

This scheme is accredited by the Leicester Open College Network. It is innovative in that it offers an accredited course that combines flexibility of content in terms of analysing women's position within society, with the opportunity to gain skills necessary to equip the student to seek the most suitable FE/HE course or job. It takes place within a supportive and friendly atmosphere and the emphasis is on response to people's different needs, whether they be linguistic, cultural or physical.

The overall aim of the scheme is to provide women with the skills and confidence to explore appropriate job opportunities. This involves looking at the skills and interests women already possess and that can be transferred to different settings, facilitated by the use of a computerised guidance programme.

The aims are:

- to develop self-confidence, positive self-image and assertiveness skills
- to help women identify and develop skills and awareness of their own potential for the job market
- to give appropriate practical skills to facilitate job applications
- to develop an awareness of the position of women in society.

This course is aimed at unwaged women. They may never have been in paid employment, or never been in paid employment outside the home. If they have been in paid employment, it may not have been for a considerable period of time for reasons of ill-ness, care of child or adult dependants or because of the state of the job market. It is for women who wish to enter or return to the job market, and who want to spend time evaluating the skills they have and identifying those they might wish to acquire.

The programme is drawn up by the tutor, but there is a degree of flexibility depending on the needs and wishes of the participants. The tutor is responsive to different needs depending on first language, culture and physical ability.

The scheme has as its central tenet the fact that all women have something to offer the world of paid employment. Thc course aims to equip them with the skills to reach this world. There will also be recognition of the fact that all women have experienced oppression of some sort and that at times this may have been particularly damaging. Women's self-esteem is constantly undermined and women's reality is denied self-expression. The course recognises this and works towards redressing the balance. By encouraging women to enter the job market, a different perspective on experience is provided.

The course provides opportunities to diminish the isolation and loneliness many women experience. These can be brought about by ill-health, lack of public transport, poverty, caring responsibilities, issues relating to language, fear of sexual or racial violence and many other reasons. There is the chance to build on the positive things women have already done in and with their lives and to see that not everything is out of their control. By enabling women to think realistically about entering the job market, issues of oppression and discrimination are inevitably addressed. Women's confidence in their abilities is supported.

Empowerment to think about oneself as part of the paid workforce involves a recognition that there is power to be shared. The course provides the opportunity for working out how to obtain, use and retain that power. All of this builds on women's strengths and experiences, reframing them as positively as possible.

Issues of equity are considered constantly, both in the way in that the course is devised (practical and financial support), and also in the positive, anti-oppressive images of women used throughout the material. These will include images of Asian women, black women, white women, women with disabilities, older women, lesbian women, women who are carers or users of services themselves. The aim is to promote the notion that women are powerful, capable and creative.

The course programme includes debate on what makes it difficult for women to participate in paid work, both because of personal misgivings and inhibitions, and because of structural hindrances. This gives the opportunity to look at the similarities and differences in women's experiences and to begin to identify those areas over which women can have control. In this way it is possible to draw up individual profiles of ability, achievement, need and immediate goals. It is highly necessary for each woman to have her own profile in order for her to feel as valued as possible, but the support provided by the group will be an essential part of the process, too. Introductory work, looking at where women are now and where they would like to be, is necessary to set the scene.

There are opportunities for careers and vocational guidance, both from the tutor, and from visiting speakers. This is supported by use of the computer and the Cascaid Adult Directions.

Content includes what makes it difficult to get out of the house in the first place, being taken seriously as a woman, how this is compounded by issues of race, age, parenthood, caring, sexuality, ability or disability; building up a positive picture of the self, recognising that everyone has qualities and skills, even if these do not receive validation from society in general; looking at aspirations and at what can be achieved realistically; coping with change as positively as possible; dealing with disappointment and criticism; dealing with fear of success and fear of failure.

There are practical exercises on decision-making, making priorities, job hunting, assessing which are the best sources of information, knowing what a potential employer might be seeking, drawing up a CV, presenting for interview, debriefing after the event, looking elsewhere if necessary. Issues of assertiveness, what this means in different cultural contexts, and self-image are discussed. There is the chance to practise assertive behaviour, taking account of the problems that this can generate in different situations.

At the end of the course, there is the chance for individual and group evaluation and to look to the future, either to paid employment possibilities, or to further courses.

5.1.4 Accreditation in the Community

WEA BRISTOL WOMEN'S BRANCH

The main aim of the scheme is to make opportunities for accreditation available to women in community settings, by offering easy access, 'stepping stone' courses. Both of the courses being offered, 'Make Your Experience Count' and 'New Opportunities for Women', are accredited through the local Open College Network. The courses are being put on in partnership with a local college, which means that the possibilities of progression for women to college courses are enhanced.

The notion of partnership is a key one, with the WEA Women's Branch, the college and local community groups each playing an important part.

The courses are put on after consultation with the local groups, to ensure that they meet women's needs. The group then provides the venue, where possible organises childcare and shares the responsibility for publicising the course and recruiting women onto it. The WEA arranges the course and liaises with both the local group and the college.

The college takes primary responsibility for the management of information and accounting back to the Further Education Funding Council. The WEA takes responsibility for liaising with the local Open College Network to organise the process of accreditation.

Enabling criteria

- The courses are put on in co-operation with local women's groups, most of which work directly with women experiencing poverty, discrimination and disadvantage in varying forms.

- The courses are locally-based, being run in the venue where the group already meets.
- Childcare is always offered, as is dependant care support.
- These courses are free to any woman on benefit or who is the unwaged dependant of someone on benefit. Otherwise women pay a small fee that is subsidised by the Branch's own funds.

Responsiveness and transferability

- The courses are put on in response to interest from women's groups in the community.
- The FEFC funding arrangements are being used to promote a collaboration between the college, the WEA and local groups who might not otherwise access this provision.
- The course design gives women the chance to access wider opportunities at the college, as well as in the community and the labour market.

5.1.5 Giving Real Opportunities to Women (GROW)

ROTHER VALLEY COLLEGE

Aims

- to recruit women who find it difficult to take up existing provision
- to co-ordinate a personal development package
- to identify placement opportunities and support the women in them
- to identify and support access to further training opportunities
- to enable women to recognise and celebrate their skills and strengths.

In practice the project works with women, recognising that they live real lives in the real world: transition, progression and change are not easy and often create negative experiences. The project is there to support women with the transitions and celebrates the journey from passivity to empowerment with them.

We work with women in their homes if necessary, waiting for them to feel confident and comfortable with us and the project. This relationship means that the experience is valuable, hence the name of the project, which the women involved felt told the story of their experience.

The project is there as a support for them; they come back to celebrate highlights, e.g. university entrance, voting for the first time, paid work. They also come back for support when they feel they need it, ensuring a real opportunity in an often negative environment.

Throughout the process the women are seen as individuals and are encouraged to take risks and 'give it a go'. These new-found skills are transferred into their lives in a variety of ways that enable the women to feel valued and look on their futures more positively.

5.1.6 Women and New Directions

CRAIGROYSTON COMMUNITY HIGH SCHOOL, EDINBURGH

Women and New Directions (WAND) provides guidance and pre-vocational education to women living in the Greater Pilton area of Edinburgh. Sponsored through the planning department of Lothian Regional Council, we operate a user-led service to women through the provision of individual guidance and informal group learning programmes. The project employs four full-time members of staff – co-ordinator, trainer, guidance/development worker, and information/administration worker.

Enabling criteria

Our service is free, and is designed to fit in with school hours and school holidays. In addition, we have a crèche for the under-fives and can also offer childcare expenses to our users when necessary. We can also organise 'pick ups' from local nurseries and schools to our crèche. Our aim is to provide high quality childcare, and we have a minimum standard to which our crèches must comply.

We are based in the local community high school and we also offer travelling expenses to women who need them. In addition, we hold sessions on an outreach basis to encourage new users. We constantly monitor our recruitment strategies which include outreach and networking, advertising in the local free newspaper, leaflet drops in schools. We hold regular Open Days where our existing users are encouraged to bring along their friends.

Responsiveness and transferability

WAND has a management committee of 15 local women, all current or recent users of the project, and this enables us to be aware of and respond to needs at a grassroots level. We have designed a range of courses, from confidence-building, options and choices, job-seeking and study skills to living in a changing community, the psychology of communication and women's studies. We are constantly developing new courses in response to demand.

We also offer ongoing individual educational and vocational guidance. This means that women who have moved on to take up other opportunities are welcome to come back at any time for further advice or support. Based in a community school, we liaise with guidance staff to enable our users to take full advantage of local education and training opportunities. The majority of our users have progressed to further or higher education, employment or activity within the community.

We have undertaken a number of joint ventures with other organisations. This has included piloting new courses with FE colleges and the OU, for example, and designing and co-tutoring courses with other agencies.

Innovation and exploration

As a project run by and for women, we feel it is important to set standards in employment practice. Staff contracts recognise domestic commitments and offer parental leave, time off for caring for sick relatives, etc. In addition, a good staff development budget has enabled all of the staff to improve on their qualifications.

The project has also developed skills in the area of management committee training and staff development and team building and has been a resource in this way to other community groups in the area.

We have also been influential in the development of good quality childcare. We made contact at the beginning of the project with a fledging local crèche co-operative whose members were all on the Enterprise Allowance Scheme. The aim was to provide good quality childcare and together we have supported each other to help raise the standard of childcare provision in our local area. This has also had the beneficial effect of increasing local employment opportunities in childcare. In addition, we have piloted after-school care provision with a grant from the local Partnership, and supported women from the local community in a successful application for Urban Aid funding for a childcare project.

We are currently developing ways to improve our service to women with disabilities and women from ethnic minorities, and to this end we are undertaking joint work with a local Access Ability project. In addition, we have recently applied for European funding for an additional guidance/development worker to develop our work with ethnic minorities.

Evaluation

We constantly monitor and evaluate our services, and have recently improved our database to facilitate this. We receive a yearly assessment from our sponsor department, and last year we developed a new management plan to take us to the end of our Urban Aid funding. We are currently exploring ways in which psychometric measurements such as self-esteem questionnaires can be used to qualitatively evaluate our service.

5.1.7 New Start and Starting Again

SUFFOLK WEST FEDERATION OF WOMEN'S INSTITUTES AND WEST SUFFOLK COLLEGE

New Start and Starting Again both share the following aims:

- to enable students to reflect on past experiences both in or out of paid employment, and to apply these reflections to their present situation
- to establish students' self-knowledge and to develop their self- confidence, particularly in relation to seeking employment
- to help students make informed and realistic decisions about their own futures including the option to regain or start paid employment
- to foster a creative approach to planning, decision-making and problem-solving and to develop effective strategies for coping with often conflicting demands on their time

- to develop job-seeking skills, especially those relating to interaction with others.

Starting Again courses run for six weeks or within one-day workshops, at a variety of rural locations in western Suffolk.

New Start is a 20-week course, run twice a year and based at West Suffolk College in Bury St Edmunds. In addition to the aims outlined above it seeks to provide up-to-date experience of vocational training and to allow students to sample three areas that are new to them or that have changed considerably since they were last in work.

Recruitment and access

- most students on these programmes are referred from Education Guidance workers based in libraries and other locations scattered around the county, careers officers, or by personal recommendation by past students
- the varied rural locations for Starting Again are designed to help women without transport, or leading busy lives, to join a group
- a crèche is provided free of charge at most of the rural venues. At College a crèche group within the nursery is available to New Start students
- there are no fees for New Start or Starting Again courses
- the timing of the courses is designed to suit women who have busy domestic lives, need to pick children up from school, and so on.

Responsiveness and transferability

- student support, encouragement and guidance is an essential and integrated part of all the course areas. New Start has a five-week introductory core concentrating on these areas, and this support continues into later elements of the course, with core tutors available to students, and meeting them on a tutorial basis. A recent FEFC inspection commented very favourably on this element of support
- the 'taster' vocational modules within New Start are designed to offer insights into work and careers in some areas traditionally of interest to women, alongside less

conventional spheres of women's employment such as technology and management
- these tasters combine a flavour of vocational course work with advice and guidance relating to job opportunities
- New Start and Starting Again students progress on to other vocational or academic courses at West Suffolk College or elsewhere.

Evaluation

Two forms of student evaluation are undertaken for New Start:

1. *On-course evaluation:* towards the end of the course evaluation sheets are distributed to students for them to consider and keep to complete. These mainly relate to the content and presentation of the core and taster units, and to students' future plans. A final one-hour session in the last week of the course is devoted to evaluation. All remaining students and staff involved in the course come together to discuss reactions to the course, and the evaluation sheets are completed
2. *Follow-up:* students who are willing are contacted approximately six months after the end of the course and asked to complete and return a questionnaire. This focuses on their work and educational activities since completing New Start and helps to provide some destination statistics for the course.

5.1.8 Rutland, Melton and Vale of Belvoir Women's Access Project

MELTON MOWBRAY COLLEGE

The Women's Access Project is based at five centres – the Vale of Catmose College in Oakham, Uppingham Community College, Casterton Community College, Melton Mowbray College of FE and Bottesford Community Centre at Belvoir High School.

Enabling criteria

Project target group

The target group is women who have had poor or limited access to education. The Project has established links with community groups and key workers who represent this group's interests, including Homestart, Adult Basic Education and Volunteer Bureaux. Recruitment is also conducted by Project outreach workers, word of mouth in the community and via other organisations such as primary schools and through the press.

Special educational needs

Women with literacy and numeracy needs are provided for via Adult Basic Education. Three of the centres have Project staff who are also ABE workers and the other two have made arrangements with the local ABE service. All centres have some disabled access and every effort is made to accommodate women with access requirements. One centre has developed access for the visually impaired. Women at Melton have access to the extensive College special needs provision and links with the Melton Mental Health Project.

Access and support

All centres provide childcare facilities with trained staff. All centres other than Melton make a set charge per woman per day, however many activities she takes part in. This sum is paid weekly. All operate a policy of never turning away a woman because she cannot afford to pay. Melton College operates the FEFC 100 per cent fee remission for those on certain benefits. Some other provision is free for all. Otherwise women pay the College rate for 20 hours of workshop time, but instead of the normal arrangement whereby students buy in to one workshop, they can use their 20 hours across College.

Learner support is an integral part of the Project. Each woman will have a guidance interview at some time in her first term and her progress will be recorded. Follow-up interviews are offered and trained educational guidance staff are available at each centre. Each centre has computer-aided guidance facilities – TAP, Microdoors and Adult Directions. As a project accredited by Leicestershire TEC (LTEC), we have a Quality Assurance framework and as part of that are working towards a minimum resources level at each centre. The environment is designed to be supportive and friendly. Project staff are often involved in advocacy and referral work on behalf of women who have other needs and problems.

Because the Project is based in a rural area, help is given with transport where possible. Two centres offer driving lessons.

All provision is run in school hours, in school term-times. The Project is based at five centres across a very large rural area (600 square miles) to facilitate access. The educational guidance service can, and often is, taken out to people's homes.

Each Project centre runs for at least two days per week and women can choose when they attend and for how long. Almost all the programme is run on a workshop basis. The Project runs on a roll-on roll-off system. These arrangements are all designed to assist women to work around other commitments and not to feel stressed if they miss sessions or under pressure to attend at particular times.

Responsiveness and transferability

The Project has a core curriculum of IT, maths and English to GCSE, assertiveness skills and educational guidance. This is designed to meet the perceived and expressed needs of the Project target group. Activities that make up the supporting curriculum must support the core curriculum (e.g. ABE) or provide initial access to the Project. The latter may include activities such as aerobics because we have found that women are more likely to take part initially in an activity that they see as non-threatening and familiar. The Project continually re-assesses need and will introduce additional provision as appropriate and where funding allows. Recent additions include NVQs in Business Administration, First Aid qualifications and Interior Design.

The new funding structures have allowed the Project to obtain mainstream FEFC funding. In response to the FEFC requirement for accreditation, the Project has set up a working group to investigate Open College accreditation for those parts of its programme not accredited elsewhere. As a result, Leicestershire Open College Network accreditation is already in place for portfolio preparation, the material for which is a requirement of the LTEC funding already acquired by the Project.

That the design of the Project's provision is transferable has already been demonstrated by the fact that originally established at Uppingham Community College, it has transferred successfully to two other Community Colleges, a High School Community Centre and an FE College. The design is very flexible and responsive and could work in a number of other situations.

The Project's intention is that women should move on, when they are ready, to paid employment, further or higher education or other areas of activity. Educational guidance is an integral part of the programme. In addition, centres run courses on job search skills and portfolio preparation and have other related activities such as speakers from particular employment areas and links with local Job Centres and the careers and guidance service.

Innovation and exploration

In the curriculum

One example is the introduction of driving lessons. We negotiated with a local woman driving instructor for her to take three women out together for five introductory sessions. The women took it in turns to drive and observe. Most of the women have gone on to take further lessons and the test. This was a direct response to the women's lack of mobility in the area. Another example is swimming lessons. The team discovered that a number of women on the Project were unable to swim. One centre negotiated time at a local public school's pool and one with its host centre's pool. Not only do women learn a new skill, but the experience is very successful in improving self-esteem and motivation to try new skill areas. Other examples include a short course on running a small business and house maintenance.

Teaching methods

The team has explored a range of teaching methods in an attempt to meet the diverse needs of the women. One example of innovation is 'Maths by distance learning', where a tutor visits the centre every four to six weeks and the rest of the tuition is done by post, using tapes and completed work. A further example is visits to local companies, where one group, for example, visited Kwikfit to receive instruction as part of a car maintenance course.

Staff development

Funding for time for staff development is a major problem. However, last year all but one educational guidance worker took advantage of the LTEC-funded RSA Diploma in Educational Guidance. Other activities have included work shadowing as part of an induction programme for a new guidance worker, whereby she accompanied an experienced member of the team. This is part of a wider 'domino system', in which individual team members take part in particular activities and then cascade the acquired information to other team members. For example, two team members are currently being paid to explore and action LOCN accreditation. The delivery of the new LOCN-accredited portfolio preparation course will be the subject of a team meeting and the two members involved have put together a tutor pack.

Evaluation

Evaluation is carried our by each centre team, by the Project team and by the Project management group. Centres use their own evaluation forms. All the Project's work is also subject to external evaluation by funders. In some cases this is evaluation by outcome. In other cases, for example LTEC-funded educational guidance, the Project is required to produce a quality assurance framework and follow up every enquirer.

5.2 Mixed and multi-purpose provision

This category did not focus on specific courses or schemes but included a range of whole-college or faculty provision that gave women a wide choice of possible re-entry and progression routes. Coupled with this choice is the need for advice and guidance on what might be appropriate, and so one example in this group emphasised the role of a specific women's guidance project and another the possibility for the Accreditation of Prior Learning. Finally there were two examples of work in Wales, one that concentrated on providing alternatives for women in coalmining areas and another that organised a series of roadshows in the valleys of South Wales, encouraging women to consider all kinds of learning opportunities.

5.2.1 Women's Course Programme

BARNSLEY COLLEGE

The scheme has excellent results, with women using the courses as a 'stepping stone' to either work or education. Many go on to higher education via pre-Access and Access courses. Others join the courses to gain confidence and improve self-esteem. For many mature women it is a chance to make friends and meet people.

Aims

The objectives of the Women's Programme are:

- to help women gain sufficient confidence, skills and information to enable them to begin new phases in their lives
- to facilitate entry to educational courses within College and entry to higher education
- to help women enter the job market or to enhance their career and re-train for another career
- to respond to the needs of women by providing responsive, varied teaching and learning approaches
- to cater for those without conventional qualifications who do not feel ready for further education or work

- to help women train in non-traditional areas of work, thereby facilitating the implementation of an Equal Opportunities policy.
- to meet the needs of specific groups in the community identified as under-represented in education or employment.

Provision

The College offers a Women's Short Course Programme ranging from two to 16 hours a week over 12 weeks.

The courses running at present are:

- assertiveness training (day and evening)
- women and society
- living and working with young children
- women return to work
- creative writing
- women and information technology
- women and health
- look after yourself
- women and maths
- introductory award in supervisory management (NEBSM).

As part of the Women Return to Work Course, students learn word-processing, job search/interview skills, careers advice and confidence-building. The course also supplies tasters in various courses in the College and a work placement is part of the course.

All the students are given individual support and guidance and counselling, and residential weekends at Northern College and regular outings are part of the programme. Links with all the Learning Workshops are also encouraged.

Accommodation

There is a Women's Room that serves as both a teaching room and a counselling room. Childcare facilities are available.

Accreditation

All students receive a College certificate on completion of the course, and Assertiveness Training and Living and Working with Young Children are accredited by SYOCF. The Women Return to

Work course is accredited by the National Examining Board in Supervisory Management.

5.2.2 Faculty of Education and Community Studies

UNIVERSITY OF READING

The Faculty of Education and Community Studies at the University of Reading has a programme of provision for women's education, and offers pathways and opportunities to women in the form of diploma, undergraduate, postgraduate and short courses. Our work takes place within an equal opportunities framework that is applied to student recruitment and retention, and service delivery. Consequently, we have considerable student diversity in terms of age, ethnicity and experience. Attention is paid to access and accreditation. Our courses lead to employment and to higher level university courses. We have good links with employing organisations and are responsive to changes and staff development requirements. We are committed to gender appropriate curriculum provision and to empowering, participative teaching methodologies in the form of group work and experiential learning. Many of our courses are vocational, with an applied focus and an excellent rate of employment on completion. Transferability of learning from university to the learning dimension of the workplace is a strength of our courses.

Course provision

The Women Achievers Programme

This specialises in providing Management and Professional Development training for women from a range of occupations in both public and private sectors. The Certificate of Management Studies: Human Resource Management offers the opportunity for women in management positions to work and learn together, once a week over 30 weeks, sharing and comparing their experiences of applying management principles to the workplace. Successful completion of this course affords access to a part-time Diploma in Management Studies. Both courses include a Return to Learning session and are modular to allow flexibility of attendance. Professional Development Courses and Management Workshops are run both as open courses and as tailor-made company training. Topics covered include team-building, leadership skills, communication and presentation skills, time management, goal setting, career planning and becoming more visible in the workplace.

BA (hons) in Community and Youth Studies & BA (hons) in Health Studies

Both these degrees have Women's Studies modules. The client groups for these courses are post-experience, black and white, mature practitioners in community projects, voluntary organisations, the youth service and the health service. Consequently, there are excellent opportunities for integrating theory and practice and for dissemination among women in the wider community. The modules include working with young women; violence against women; language, gender and power; feminist theory; the gendered psyche; cultural representation; sexuality; black women; women and health; reproductive technology; the body; disability awareness; community development; women and education.

MA in Equity and Change in Public Services

This new degree has an emphasis on the principles and practice of equity in public service organisations. There is a module on Women into Management, and strong support for the degree from Opportunity 2000. This postgraduate provision offers women the opportunity to develop skills and knowledge that will enable them to participate, at senior levels, in management and organisational development in the public services.

Agricultural Extension Development

This department runs a programme of courses for women in developing countries. The Women in Agricultural Development is a three-month course that includes topics on approaches to the involvement of women in the process of change, issues and technologies related to women's involvement in agriculture; food; nutrition and health; strategies and methods for working with rural women and appraisal of basic technologies to develop key rural practices. This course attracts participants from countries including Dominique, St Lucia, Sierra Leone, Iraq, Ethiopia, Bangladesh and China.

Enabling criteria

Participation of women is considered in recruitment and selection, with advertisements in a range of community publications, as well as local newspapers across three counties. Recruitment and selection is also conducted within an equal opportunities framework, with an emphasis on valuing wider experience and potential, as well as academic qualifications. Student bursaries are available.

We have a good support system for students with special needs, including interpreters for students with hearing disabilities. The university employs a Study Skills Officer, who provides group and individual tuition to support the academic development of non-traditional students. There is also an Academic Development Module, which offers non-traditional students a distance learning course on study skills. There is an extensive student services system, incorporating welfare, counselling and careers guidance.

Crèche facilities are available, with additional provision for half-term holidays.

Evaluation

The faculty employs a system of quality assurance that incorporates student and employer evaluation. This material is fed into course development and management.

Innovation and exploration

The faculty has received international acclaim for its research and development in education. There is particular expertise and a good publication record in equal opportunities, gender and education, evaluation, feminist theory, mature students' learning styles and pedagogy for empowerment with non-traditional students in higher education.

The faculty has expert status at the Equal Opportunities Unit of the European Union, Brussels, for its Women's Studies programme with non-traditional women students in Community and Youth Studies. The programme has been commended for its student diversity and use of group process.

The faculty offers students the possibility of studying abroad under the ERASMUS/Inter-Collegiate Programme. This allows students to study in partner European institutions or to undertake fieldwork abroad for a period of three months.

5.2.3 Women's Guidance Project

NELSON AND COLNE COLLEGE

Aims

- to provide guidance and support for women at times and in places that are convenient to them
- to facilitate the return of women to education and training
- to respond to women's needs on an individual basis.

The College has combined the role of educational guidance worker with that of community activitist; guidance has been attached to a proactive role in the community.

Background to the submission

The college has worked intensively with women of Asian heritage for a number of years, specifically in the area of English language acquisition, and more recently in the delivery of courses designed to enable access to vocational education and training.

This provision has taken three main forms, each designed to facilitate attendance, according to the women's circumstances. These forms are:

- home tuition on a one-to-one basis in women's homes
- small house groups, that give a non-threatening introduction to learning in groups to the women concerned
- community-based provision, with childcare that doubles as a context in which women who so wish can learn about the importance, role and function of play for small children.

The decision was taken to extend the best aspects of this provision to all women, combining a women-only course with the provision of guidance at times and places suitable to women.

European Social Fund application

A successful submission was made to the European Social Fund. Thus it was that in June 1992, a 'New Opportunities for Women' project was started which combined the following elements:

- a one-year, full-time women-only course in Environmental Conservation, leading to a nationally recognised qualification
- free childcare provision to run alongside the course
- a 'Women's Guidance Worker', appointed to the college to give impartial advice and guidance, but who combined this with the role of marketing the course to interested groups and individuals.

Women's guidance worker

What made this post particularly significant was the fact that the worker not only organised appointment-only sessions at community venues where childcare was provided; she also visited established groups, such as voluntary bodies and community classes, and provided counselling sessions in women's own homes. The 'Home Tuition' and 'House Groups' concepts were therefore transferred into a guidance context.

The post combined the role of guidance provider with that of community activism in support of women; groups were convened in homes and community venues, group counselling and guidance was provided, and women gained self-confidence by discussing their ideas and aspirations in a supportive context.

Specific advertised sessions were offered throughout the Pendle area, and these were publicised separately in the localities concerned, as well as in a widely-distributed 'NOW' booklet. The Guidance Worker used Community Centres, Job Centres, Job Clubs and College buildings. Talks and presentations were also given about the service, not only to the statutory agencies, but also to women's groups.

Monitoring

Extensive monitoring took place throughout the duration of the project. Indeed, so successful was the project that the college decided to make the post permanent. The Women's Guidance Worker is now an integral part of the Student Services team, dividing her time between outreach work in the community, making appointments on college premises, and administering a college-based fund devoted exclusively to helping defray students' childcare costs.

After each counselling session or interview, documentation on every women was recorded; 370 women were seen over a two-year period, and a questionnaire was completed itemising: age; education/qualifications; ethnic origin; current situation; previous employment; aspirations; destinations; follow-up interview, if required.

Seventy-four per cent of the women interviewed wanted education/training or retraining to update skills/qualifications that would facilitate their entry into the employment market or higher/further education. Seventeen per cent of the women followed other destinations that included employment, target training, Job Club or self-employment. Nine per cent required a follow-up interview having considered their options in the intervening months.

The high percentage of successfully placed women whose declared needs were for training/retraining indicates the measure of achievement of this initiative.

Support

Women who were placed on college courses were able to return to the Guidance Worker for ongoing support. This support was also an integral part both of the Environmental Conservation Course ('NOW 1') as well as 'NOW 2', a one-year, full-time women-only course in Supervisory Management. This later course built upon the success of 'NOW 1'. Because of the European funding obtained, it was possible to offer these courses free to women, as well as provide free childcare.

Conclusion

Nelson and Colne College believes that its Women's Guidance Worker post builds on previous good practice, because:

- it facilitates women's return to study, training or work by ensuring that they are placed on education or training programmes that suit them
- it encourages the participation of women in programmes by having a flexible approach to the time and place of guidance interviews

- it facilitates access to childcare provision by the administration and deployment of a childcare fund for adult students
- it provides ongoing support for women
- it is responsive to the needs of women
- monitoring, by statistical analysis, has been an integral part of the project.

5.2.4 APL Project

HACKNEY COMMUNITY COLLEGE

Aims

- to target women in the workforce in order to accredit prior knowledge and skills
- to accredit or partially accredit women's unpaid work, particularly childcare experience
- to raise the confidence of women, particularly those who are unemployed, refugees and ethnic minorities, or those with disabilities
- to award credit to women.

The way these aims are implemented is demonstrated in the following selections from the course leaflet.

What is APL?

APL stands for Accreditation of Prior Learning. That means it is possible for you to get credit for the skills, knowledge and achievements you have gained from work, leisure or other activities. The credit you are given could lead to a nationally recognised qualification, help you to get a job or go onto a course you've always wanted to do. For example, if you are returning to education after spending years bringing up a family, the skills you have acquired may help you get a qualification, train for a new career, or get onto a course.

Prior experience

When we look back at what we've done in our lives, it's difficult to imagine how our experience could possibly be recognised. That's where APL comes in. We are here to help you match your ambitions with your past experiences. There's really no reason why everybody shouldn't get credit for what they already know and improve their prospects.

Qualifications

It may be possible for you to get credit for your past experience from well-known accrediting bodies (such as City & Guilds) and there are more and more subjects being covered, so don't think you've been left out. Come and talk to us first and you may find that you're more qualified than you think!

What is involved?

Firstly, you will need to come and talk to one of our guidance workers who will discuss your particular ambitions in order to establish the best possible route for you to take. You will also be asked about your skills, qualification and work experience, so it would be useful if you brought any papers you have that you think might be relevant to the interview. If APL is not the best way forward, we will recommend alternatives.

Overseas students

If you have arrived with qualifications from abroad, it may be possible for you to get your qualifications and work cxperience recognised in this country. Come and find out!

Make APL work for you

There's really no reason why we can't all have a bite of the APL. It doesn't matter where you are from, what you do and what you did. If a lack of qualifications has prevented you from getting what you want out of life, then we may be able to help. Get in touch.

5.2.5 Women in the Workforce: Alternative Choices for Women from Coalmining Areas

DOVE WORKSHOP, NEATH

The DOVE Workshop, based at Banwen Community Centre, is a community education provider organised by women and based in a village in a mining community in South Wales.

The training project identifies under-represented women living in the coalmining communities in the Dulais, Neath and Swansea valleys who need training in intermediate information technology and supervisory management skills. The course offers a progression route from a Women in Technology course to a module in Computer Science available from further and higher education providers in the Community Centre. However, other progression routes are available according to individual needs and the needs of the local labour market.

Women who are identified as single parents or with a low income have the opportunity to gain qualifications in management with the Institute of Supervisory Management, credits with the South West Wales Open College and Access Consortium and NVQs where appropriate. Guidance and counselling form an integral part of the course alongside crèche and transport support. The DOVE workshop works closely with the guidance unit at the Department of Adult and Continuing Education, University College Swansea. Also based at the Banwen Community Centre is a study skills programme and library networked to the South Wales Miners' Library. With the support of an Equal Opportunities policy the course offers a flexible learning programme for trainees using all facilities.

The project is part of a transnational partnership with other training organisations in existing or former coalmining areas in Europe. This transnational link enables women from the four coalfield areas to exchange relevant course documents, to communicate through exchange visits, and seminars and to communicate through telecommunications, taking into account shared similarities and diverse differences.

The project is able to compare and contrast, within a European perspective, the socio-economic, cultural and political factors affecting women who seek to enter the workforce. The project's research will study the impact of industrial change and the effect on women within these specific factors.

5.2.6 The Valley's Women's Roadshow

RISCA, GWENT

Glenys Kinnock MEP writes:

The Valley's Women's Roadshow organises, in partnership with local women and education providers, 'fun days' for women in the communities throughout the South Wales Valleys. These 'fun days' are a combination of workshops, guidance, information and exhibitions. They provide women with the opportunity to try out a wide range of activities such as DIY, Languages for Beginners, Beauty Therapy, Car Maintenance, Play Activities, Creative Writing, Computing, etc. Staff are on hand to offer guidance and a variety of organisations have stands or exhibits at the events.

The roadshow's aims are:

- to raise awareness of training and educational opportunities for women
- to highlight needs and barriers
- to support and encourage women in gaining access to learning opportunities
- to work in partnership to widen opportunities for women.

The Valley's Roadshow aims to achieve this by:

- researching existing provision
- identifying unmet need
- organising events focusing on women
- providing an extensive information service
- setting up local networking groups.

The Valleys Women's Roadshow removes many of thc barriers that prevent women returning to education and is committed to providing a service that is woman-centred.

A crèche is provided at the events, which are always organised when children are in school, during school hours. There is no charge to attend the days, apart from a small charge for refreshments. All the venues are fully accessible and transport is provided if that is a problem.

The Valleys Women's Roadshow is all too aware that a lack of confidence is a major psychological barrier to women returning to education. The emphasis with their events is on having fun and the atmosphere is informal and friendly. The 'Fun Days' give women the opportunity to try out activities in a friendly, non-threatening atmosphere and to experiment before committing themselves to a particular subject.

The Valleys Women's Roadshow actually takes their events to the women they are trying to attract by holding events in the heart of their communities. In addition, it is *local women* that set the agenda. Prior to each event, the Valleys Women's Roadshow holds meeting with local women and education providers in the area.

This ensures that the workshops they organise are ones that will appeal to local women and that reflect the culture of their community.

All promotional/publicity materials that are distributed before the event reflect the Valley Women's Roadshow's commitment to equal opportunities and promote positive images of women.

Since knowing where to go for information can in itself be a barrier for women, advice and guidance is an integral part of each 'Fun Day'. The staff offer advice and information and have access to a database of educational opportunities in that area. The Valleys Women's Roadshow has a referral process that assists women to access the educational opportunities they are interested in.

The Valleys Women's Roadshow is sensitive to the needs of all women, including those with learning difficulties or who may be lacking in basic skills. The wide variety of workshops, many of which are practical ones such as DIY, mean that there is something for everyone and no one need feel 'out of their depth'. The use of traditional and non-traditional workshops is also important, enabling women who feel able to try something different such as French for Beginners to do so, while less confident women can join in workshops on subjects with which they are familiar, and feel comfortable, such as Playskills, 'Healthy Eating on a Budget' or Hair and Beauty.

One of the great strengths of the Valleys Women's Roadshow is its collaborative style of working, as all events are a real partnership between local women, community groups, and educational providers. This means that information about the barriers to education, training and employment faced by women are raised with education providers. Also, as each event is carefully evaluated from the perspective of the women who attend the event and that of the partners, it ensures that the Valleys Women's Roadshow has a basis from which to improve their working practice and influence the provision of educational and training opportunities in South Wales.

The Valleys Women's Roadshow is committed to researching the opportunities for progression for women and to recording the progression routes and developments from events. Women who attend one of the 'Fun Days' are given tracking cards that they then return when they take up any educational activities. This is a unique way of monitoring the progress of women.

The follow-up of events is, of course, an important aspect of the work of the Valleys Women's Roadshow. Where interest has been shown at one of the events, information and guidance are made available to ensure that the woman's interest is maintained and that the progression to courses is as easy as possible for her.

I launched the Valleys Women's Roadshow and have been very impressed by the progress it has made since its launch. I have seen the Roadshow in action and have seen how effective and successful its 'Fun Days' for women are in different parts of my constituency. I certainly believe that the confidence I felt when I launched it has been fully justified.

5.2.7 Women's Resource and Development Agency

BELFAST

The Women's Resource and Development Agency (WRDA) works across Northern Ireland. We aim to:

- enhance the lives of women by promoting positive change
- facilitate action through addressing the social, economic and political factors that affect women
- empower women to take positive action in their lives
- promote the growth of self-esteem, motivation, skills and the authority of women.

How are women enabled?

WRDA believes that learning takes place within a social, economic and political context, and that this should be made explicit. This belief determines choices about where we work, the way in which we make contact with women, and what happens once we have made contact. We share with other adult and community education practitioners a commitment to understanding and removing barriers to access. We also draw on community development practice and feminism, in an effort to enhance the lives of individual women so that they may also choose to make a wider contribution to their communities.

In essence this means that local women are encouraged to develop themselves and their community as part of a process that seeks actively to promote the equality of women in all aspects of society.

A recent review led to a re-affirmation of our commitment to combining work on three fronts: feminism, community development and education. Rather than dilute the impact of each, reflection indicates that each element is a necessary and inseparable part of the whole.

This three-stranded approach works on the premise that the potential and capacity for change and development in women's lives exists, but needs to be activated by an educational experience that is relevant and accessible in their everyday lives, i.e. in their communities.

Responsive to the needs of women?

This is an issue that we are currently re-examining. We believe there is a balance to be struck between recognising the importance of listening to what women say they want, and recognising that women may express needs on the basis of limited information. Too close a reliance on responding to expressed need therefore will make us ineffective in our role of enlarging that range of opportunities open to women.

We are in the early stages of piloting an introductory module that would give women the opportunity to analyse how they come to make decisions about what they would like to learn, what style of learning suits them best, and alternative pathways and directions they could explore as adult learners. This process would aim to improve the quality of decisions women make and to give them confidence to voice their needs and preferences.

Our long-term aim would be to develop a programme that could be adapted to suit different situations, could be accredited, and could, in another form, be included in staff development for community workers.

We are actively involved in developing, sustaining and participating in networks of women's groups. For example, a group in East Belfast, having organised and published a research programme, now has to deal with the response generated by its success, and attempt to retain ownership of the process as statutory agencies move in. We will work with the women to support them, developing appropriate training, and accrediting this where possible and wanted.

Responsive and transferable

WRDA is a small organisation with limited resources and most of our funding is for projects. We have to think carefully about how to maximise these resources in a way that most benefits disadvantaged women. Our policy at the moment is to work towards a 'training the trainers' approach which seeks to identify key women in communities, often participants in learning programmes, and through training and support to develop them as tutors/facilitators. We hope this will lead to an increased interest and awareness in education and training opportunities at the grassroots.

This way of working is facilitated by the presence in Northern Ireland of an active movement of women at a grassroots level where organisations enjoy relative stability of membership. This allows us to see real progression over time, so that a woman who once became involved at the level of participating in a confidence building group may now be facilitating a similar process herself. In the longer term, this same woman might be using her experience to inform decisions affecting policy and resource allocation in her local area, or at a city-wide level.

Innovative?

A key characteristic of our approach is outreach: locally-based activities that are flexibly arranged, giving women planning and control of activities. We promote women-only courses and discussions, and use a range of teaching styles.

The pedagogical approach is concerned more with collective than personal development, but by developing individual women's confidence, judgement, initiative, organisational abilities and creativity and encouraging them to work as a team the project assists them to make a wider contribution to the group and their communities. All activities aim to foster greater confidence, self-esteem and assertiveness and are directed at increasing a group's skills and building up its resources and are as much about process as content.

We believe that the approach of empowerment and support that we practise in work with local communities should be mirrored within the organisation. Supervision and team meetings are prioritised, staff are supported to take time off in lieu before the build-up of such time gets out of proportion. Staff development costs are included in all fundraising applications. We aim to develop models of good practice in all aspects of our work and to value our workers. We therefore provide all our workers with comprehensive contracts and fair salaries based on the Joint National Council scale. We have also recently introduced a pension scheme.

Evaluation

Evaluation takes place on three levels: the organisation, individual projects, and courses. These internal processes are complemented by externally conducted evaluation exercises at regular intervals.

We believe in evaluation as a means of analysing our effectiveness, but additionally as a measure of accountability between the staff and management committee, the organisation and women's groups with whom we work, the tutor and participants, the project and its funders.

5.3 Parenting and childcare

There is no natural home for this type of provision in any of the previous categories, and it contains two different types of learning opportunity. The first sub-group focuses on provision for parents, primarily but not exclusively mothers, where they are offered a learning opportunity that centres on their child or children. Such provision is mainly located in schools or play areas, and encourages parents to become involved in their own as well as their children's learning.

5.3.1 Informal Learning – Life Skills, Rhondda

HAFOD PRIMARY SCHOOL, MID GLAMORGAN

At present there are 27 life skills classes in the Rhondda, Cynon, Taff Area that provide informal learning opportunities. Funding for these classes is secured by the Local Education Authority via Community Education, the Further Education Funding Council for Wales, and also by joint funding initiatives with organisations such as Save the Children and Borough Council Leisure Services.

The aim of the groups is to encourage participation by those people within the community who would not normally access formal education. Members of the groups gain confidence and self-esteem, as well as a sense of enjoyment through informal learning.

The ultimate aim with the groups is to encourage and assist clients to progress towards entry into 'access in' classes at local colleges – Aberdare, Pontypridd and Rhondda. This means working closely with the college staff and adult guidance service to provide the support needed to encourage groups to move forward.

The classes, which are offered free of charge, are held in areas that are recognised as deprived areas, where lack of public transport, pre-school childcare and low self-esteem within communities are the norm. Life skills classes are for many the first link in the chain towards further education, helping to raise awareness and building confidence.

The Trehafod Life Skills group that meets at the Hafod Primary School in the Village of Trehafod situated between Porth and Pontypridd regularly attracts 15 women in their early twenties and thirties. The class has offered them the opportunity to develop computer skills, funded by the TEC and organised by Penygraig Community Project.

These skills have to be put into practice through further opportunities offered by the Primary School, whereby members of the group could act as volunteers assisting primary school children in the Computer Class.

To further develop skills we, as a group, offered our services to re-write the School Governors' Report in 'user friendly language'. This task was completed and the finished booklet is attractive and easy to read and has been well received by the Rhondda Education Governors' Support Officer, who has requested that it be circulated throughout the Rhondda Schools as an example of good practice.

Our next venture is to produce a magazine entitled *Hafod Past and Present*. This is to be a twice-yearly publication and the profits from the sale will go to school funds. Our method has been to divide ourselves into teams consisting of people who want to use computers; those who want to develop communication skills within an advertising team (e.g. selling advertising space to local businesses); using communication and negotiating skills; and information gathering by collecting the items for publication.

The school held a competition to design a school logo and we had the help of an artist living in Llantrisant who guided the children and judged the winner. He is now helping the women's group to draw the outline of the front of the school, which is an interesting Victorian building dating back to 1882, and this we will use on all our covers, along with the new logo.

Childcare has been available for all the sessions, enabling the group to give their full attention to the project. There are six children present, all under three, who are looked after by a qualified NNEB-trained person. The school has been very co-operative in allowing us to use the school computers. Special thanks must go to the IT Manager, for his offer to use the computers at the Penygraig Project, and the TEC. As a result of this project we now have adult basic education through the use of computers as a separate class at Hafod Primary School on Tuesday afternoons. This will assist the group to produce the magazine. The finished results will have given the group the opportunity to use newly-learnt skills through working towards a finished product. As a result, a team approach has also developed, with all members making a valid contribution.

5.3.2 Parent Introductory Course

BOURNVILLE COLLEGE OF FURTHER EDUCATION

The first 10 weeks of the course offer mothers the chance to learn more about their children's schooling, e.g. talks from Parent Governors, Head Teachers, etc. The second 10 weeks focus upon parents as individuals. The College arranges for speakers from all units to chat to parents about their vocational aspirations. They are all offered exit counselling. So far, all participants have progressed to a range of courses and programmes.

The first 10 weeks are held in the various schools, with refreshments and childcare provided. The second 10 weeks are held in college, also with free childcare.

Each student is offered group and individual tutorial sessions and action plans are drawn up.

The completing students attend a presentation, where college certificates are presented by the Principal.

The roots of this programme are fixed firmly within the community . Eighteen local schools are involved on an on-going basis. Some of the schools are in areas of prime deprivation, one of them being in the top two per cent of national statistics. The growing awareness of mothers that they can change their current situation through education comes throughout the programme. Access to the college counsellor and full college facilities, e.g. Open Learning, Library, etc., is also made available

5.3.3 Fair Play Training and Development Project

MID-CRAIGIE, DUNDEE

The main aim is to promote positive play practices by offering a wide variety of training/learning opportunities particularly for women, many unemployed, many traditional non-participants, many young lone parents. For most this is their first entry into informal adult education. We have evidence to show that the vast majority of adults who are introduced to informal training by us find it a very positive experience. Many go on to further training, some gain enough confidence to enter the job market and tend to find employment, usually as part-time crèche workers, child minders or youth workers.

Examples of good, innovative practice

- the handouts for a creche course being run specifically for Dundee International Women's Centre are being translated into Gujerati
- another course is planned to take place in the sitting-room of a residential home for single mothers
- we pay for the provision of crèche workers (trained by us) where necessary
- well-illustrated Distance Learning materials on play have been produced in language not off-putting to adult returners
- we are in the process of becoming a centre approved by SCOTVEC to offer SVQs in Playwork. This will enhance the job prospects for many of our participants
- all sessions and courses are evaluated by staff and various methods of feedback are used to collect comments from trainees.

Extracts from our Annual Report give examples of clients' comments.

After Crèche Workers' Training:

'Time was taken to explain anything that wasn't understood at first. The trainers are very nice people to work with so this made the course even more interesting and enjoyable.'

'The time we had on the course learned me a lot of things I would never have thought about otherwise.'

'I've never had a certificate before. I'm going to get it framed.'

After Youth Workers' Training:

'Good tutoring, good sessions, great way to learn. All the trainings were relevant to our club.'

'It was things I never did before.'

After Playschemes Training:

'I enjoyed the camaraderie of a bunch of people with similar aims, co-operating and swapping ideas.'

'Most of all I've enjoyed the team spirit of the day training and also found the unselfconscious enthusiasm of the persons running the training infectious. Halfway through the first game we were a room full of friends rather than strangers.'

'I enjoyed the whole day, everyone was friendly and mixed well, not for a while have I acted like a kid and not felt stupid.'

'Brilliantly done – well done again Fair Play!'

After Summer Project Training:

'I got to try painting my own face at the Day of Play.'

'It's a Knockout organised by Fair Play was just brilliant. We all got really wet!'

'The support we got from Fair Play was really appreciated.'

5.4 Parents and learning: Accredited courses

This sub-group also has its roots in parents' involvement in their children's learning and is one indication of a growing trend. We know that courses for playgroup workers and volunteers have opened up educational opportunities and a route back into learning for countless women. For many years mothers have helped out in the classroom, often untrained and unpaid but a valuable resource. Some have used that experience to move on to other work with children. So while the growth of the new courses for 'classroom assistants' can be viewed with some suspicion as a cheap way of reducing the need for trained teachers, it is providing many women with an opportunity to improve their qualifications, and in turn may lead to further progresion routes.

Another route to qualifications that has also been developed recently is via the acquisition of NVQs in childcare and education. The progression possibilities and the employment potential for women gaining this qualification have yet to be tested, but, in some cases, it is already providing high quality training.

5.4.1 Classroom Assistant Training

MID-KENT COLLEGE OF FURTHER AND HIGHER EDUCATION

Many women work in school as classroom assistants. They often have school-age children of their own and can fit their working hours around their children's school-time. They are often given a great deal of responsibility within the school, e.g. working with pupils with special educational needs, yet usually have no commensurate level of pay and training, or a recognised career structure and progression. The classroom assistant training course at Mid-Kent College was therefore set up to try to provide:

- professional recognition for women working as classroom assistants
- a quality training course
- a qualification

- a route (through the CATS system) into higher education or teacher training for those students who wish to carry on.

The course is based on a new pilot scheme run by RSA, but the curriculum has been written specifically to provide both for experienced classroom assistants and those new to schools, e.g. parent helpers or people following Training for Work schemes.

There are no official entry qualifications. Although the DfEE would like all candidates to have GCSE English and maths, most classroom assistants do not have both these qualifications, so learning support has been built into the course for maths and English.

Support for special needs is also built into the course, and much of the course content is concerned with pupils with special educational needs, including hearing and visual impairment, emotional behavioural difficulties, autism, specific learning difficulties, and physical and medical problems.

Course hours are fixed to harmonise with 9.30 am to 2.30 pm during term-time to enable students to take their children to school and collect them afterwards.

Traditionally most classroom assistants have to undertake training in their own time. This course is run as day release to emphasise its importance to employers. Heads and teachers are invited in to regular presentation evenings so that they are fully aware of the course content and delivery.

Also provided are:

- a classroom assistant mentor/facilitator
- study skills for those students returning to learning after a long period at home looking after children
- guidance and counselling.

The course is evaluated constantly and feedback is sought from the students so that teaching and learning strategies can be altered to be more effective and to meet the needs of the students.

The course runs for 20 weeks and costs £275. Most students are funded by schools, which shows a level of commitment on the part of local schools to classroom assistant training. The college operates a concessionary fee policy and students on benefits have their fees paid. Some students fund themselves.

This all sounds rather dry, but we also aim to make the course interesting, challenging and fun!

5.4.2 Access to Childcare and Education NVQs

DAN-Y-COED EDUCATION AND TRAINING SERVICES

The programme is considered to be innovative for the following reasons.

Dan-y-Coed Education and Training Centre was the first City & Guilds Approved Examination Centre for the Childcare and Education NVQ Level 2 in the South Wales area. The Centre has also been the first, certainly within the county of West Glamorgan, to produce successful candidates both in private day nursery and county Primary School settings.

The project seeks to provide access to the Childcare and Education NVQ to a group of 10 adult candidates. Funding has been obtained from the West Wales TEC to support the initiative.

A key feature of the project is the use of an open learning package. Two packages are available. Both are extremely new. *Working with Children*, developed by the Open College, became available in September. *Children First*, developed by the National Extension College, is so new that a copy was forwarded to Dan-y-Coed by express delivery for use in an awareness-raising evening.

The project will be evaluated to assess the opportunity of cascading the programme to a wider market in the West Glamorgan area.

The project combines flexibility of delivery with evening guidance sessions, peripatetic assessment and open learning in a way that we feel is innovative and different, certainly for our area. We have received an enthusiastic response from those who attended our awareness-raising evening and are now looking forward to working with a range of candidates from a variety of settings that will include schools, playgroups, social services day nurseries, private day nurseries and childminding establishments.

5.5 Innovative ideas

Finally there was a set of submissions that did not fit easily into any other category because their distinctive characteristic was that they had designed innovatory provision in response to specific need. Whilst there were many other submissions that showed exciting new developments and could be classified in the same way, the five in this section were distinctive. Not all were new – the course working with groups of women has been established for several years and yet still manages to meet new challenges in a developmental way. Another group of women have developed dramatically through the writers' workshops in their local library, producing an anthology of their work, whilst another group learn and develop through outings and travel.

The two final examples are responses to a very real need – that of contributing to women's safety. Whilst one offers provision to women who are themselves fearful, the other provides a 'training the trainers' course in self defence. Self defence in itself may not remove the danger and the fear faced by many women but it may increase the confidence needed to enable women to move on to other opportunities and challenges in education and training – or indeed in their everyday lives.

5.5.1 Skills for Women Project

EX-HAREHILLS MIDDLE SCHOOL, LEEDS

Skills for Women is a women's education project established in 1986 to enable women community activists to maximise their work in the community and also to increase their confidence in order to make their demands on the decision-making process. Our target group is women with little or no post-16 education in areas of high social need. The project has a city-wide brief and works in partnership with all appropriate agencies, both statutory and voluntary. Since its inception, the project has responded to the needs of women in the community by broadening the range of courses from personal effectiveness and running community groups, to longer, more formal courses. We are trying to offer community progression routes to women as well as supporting informal groups and community activity.

Curriculum

- group skills
- committee skills
- confidence-building
- where to next?
- oppression awareness
- parents/children/schools
- women's keep safe
- coping with teenagers
- informal women's groups
- women's lives today
- foundation course.

Enabling criteria

As Skills for Women is a project of good practice we try to break down all barriers affecting women returning to education:

- courses and good quality childcare are free
- community-based wherever women feel comfortable
- length and time negotiated with women, taking into account timetables of schools and nurseries
- publicity: word of mouth, outreach and development, contacting all relevant agencies working in the community, backed up with accessible written information, in community languages if appropriate
- setting: safe, informal, friendly, creating the environment to build an effective, trusting and supportive group
- learning: student-centred, experiential and encouraging study skills
- tutors: all our tutors are experienced in informal student-centred methods. The project is able to respond to requests for community languages or bi-lingual input. Our tutor pool is mixed in terms of ethnic origin, age, class and (dis)ability
- learner support: support is built into the courses. In addition, being attached to a college means that the

guidance and support services are available when requested.

Responsiveness and transferability

All courses are negotiated. Before the course begins, a co-ordinator negotiates with a group and a course is tailor-made to the group's needs – the curriculum can be mixed and matched. One course may evolve into another, e.g. an informal confidence-building course may progress to a longer, accredited foundation course.

Because we are now a well-established project, we have built up over the years an ongoing relationship with a number of centres. As their circumstances and personnel change over time, so does our input. For example, we have been working intermittently over the past six years with the Milun Centre for Asian Women in Leeds. Initially we responded to a request from its co-ordinators to offer a course on meeting skills for the Management Committee. Some time later we returned to work with Centre users on a bi-lingual course: Parents/Children/Schools. Currently we are back in the Centre offering a confidence-building course to a largely different group of students. There are similar examples from community centres, nurseries and women's groups from across Leeds.

New funding mechanisms and structures have encouraged the project to look at individual progression routes and accreditation. Skills for Women courses are in the process of being incorporated into a modular framework that will be accredited by the Open College Network.

Courses are designed so that groups can be in control of their own learning. The groups may progress together to more structured and demanding courses, or individuals may feel they have the confidence to progress on their own, whether it be academically, vocationally or into greater involvement in the community. All courses offer an element of guidance to individuals and, where appropriate, we request that college support services visits groups.

OCN accreditation means that students, if they wish, will be able to transfer their credits to other learning situations. Moreover, the Project has excellent links with the adult education services and, where appropriate, would transfer a group or individuals into that sector. We have good relations with main site further education and are working to reduce the gap between community-based women's education courses and provision within college.

Innovation and exploration

Skills for Women has responded to women's changing needs by broadening the curriculum, delivering subject areas at various levels and ensuring that the FEFC-led move towards accreditation can be utilised to our students' advantage.

The project will work with any agency that gives us access to new women in the community. For instance, we are currently delivering courses in partnership with the Salvation Army, a hostel for homeless women and an Asian women's centre. We are also working with health workers, social services nurseries, independent community centres, youth and community services, playgroups, schools, etc.

Our innovative work tries to maintain a balance between supporting women's community activity and encouraging educational progress. However, the two are usually intertwined.

Although our curriculum areas have been broadened and can be at different levels of attainment, our ethos and philosophy remain the same. We continue to deliver courses using the same teaching methods and trying to ensure total accessibility for women.

In Leeds, the project is a resource for all women working with women, and we will share our knowledge with anyone who wishes. We have delivered various staff development events promoting good practice in community-based women's work. Currently we are working with Leeds Women's Self Defence Association to set up a training the trainers accredited course on Keeping Safe issues for women. We are waiting to see whether we will receive funding for this from the Safer Cities Programme. There is a demand for community-based 'Keep Safe' courses; however, there is a lack of qualified staff to deliver training.

Evaluation

The project has strict evaluation and monitoring procedures plus weekly ongoing support from the co-ordinators.

Tutors submit after negotiation with a group a syllabus, the course is evaluated weekly with a co-ordinator, session plans must be submitted, plus a report. Whenever possible tutors come together to review their work. All resources and materials are shared.

For students there is an assessment of needs at the beginning of the course, encouraging the students to evaluate their own learning and the group's progression, and at the end of the course there is an individual and a group evaluation exercise. The co-ordinators also evaluate the course with any worker who is providing support for the group.

One of the tutors' roles is to discuss with the group what they aim to do next – be it more of our provision, general adult education or becoming a campaigning group. Many women's groups have of necessity become self-programming and we give them as much support as possible.

We are constantly communicating with women and women's workers in order to identify how we may accommodate changing needs. The project's structure should be able to evolve with the changing environment so long as women-only education is tolerated.

5.5.2 Craigneuk and Petersburn Women Writers' Workshop

PETERSBURN LIBRARY, AIRDRIE

Aims

Craigneuk and Petersburn Women Writers' Workshop aims to guide, support and develop women's writing as a source of creativity and a means of expression. It aims to develop confidence and self-esteem in the writers.

The group was established following a very successful day-school, 'Women Write Now', held in September 1992. Three workshops examined writing from experience, poetry and short stories. The day was free with lunch and crèche provided. Around 40 women attended.

There was great support for a Women Writers' Workshop to emerge from the day. Many of the women involved had already participated in a local women's group, Women in the Arts Group involving theatre visits and literary discussions, and a Women, Writing and Culture course, all organised by Community Education.

The Writers' Workshop has built on and extended this core and welcomes new members on a weekly basis. Two years on, the average attendance at the fortnightly workshops is 20 women. A full programme of events is organised including visits from novelists and poets.

November 1993 saw the launch of the group's first anthology *Wummin's Wurds: Classy Burds*, now in its third reprint and still going strong. The range and quality of writing continues to grow.

Linked to the Women Writers' Workshop have been daytime courses on creative writing. Further offshoots hosted by the library with the same core group members include a certificated Higher English course run for the first time this year, and a Junior Writers' Workshop aimed at 8–13-year-olds and meeting in the library on Saturday morning. The Women Writers' Workshop has been a springboard for all of this.

Next on the agenda is a drama and writing day entitled 'Stages', which will bring together members of the community interested in performing and the thriving body of writers. This, like the Women Write Now day that launched the Writers' Workshop, may prove the stimulus for a new group. Again lunch and crèche will be provided on the day.

In an area with very limited amenities, high unemployment and a high percentage of lone parents, the Writers' Workshop has been a guiding light, and a joy for all who have experienced its warm, supportive atmosphere.

5.5.3 Trekkers Travel Club

THE POWER HOUSE, CARDIFF

The aim of the scheme is to broaden the horizons of female participants geographically and educationally. A heavily subsidised crèche supports all provision. The group has visited local places of historical interest, festivals and other celebrations and the theatre. Visits have taken place to France and Spain and activities have included a day on the Taff Cycle Trail and an Outdoor Activities day at the Storey Arms Outdoor Education centre.

Group members have worked at different levels to suit individual needs, but planning, map-reading and financial management have been high on the agenda, although confidence-building and empowerment have been a continuous underlying theme.

There have been various successful outcomes for group members:

- Janet has completed County Play Training courses and is currently participating in the NVQ level 3 course in Childcare
- Mary has now qualified as an HGV driver
- Joan, at 53 years of age, has left British shores for the first time and is now studying French
- Angela has recently completed her Numberpower Stage 1 at the Open Learning Centre, also housed in this building
- Joyce has successfully obtained funding to follow a two-year full-time aromatherapy and massage course and will open her own private practice.

The Trekkers scheme is being submitted for accreditation by the Open College Network to ensure access to Schedule 2 funding.

5.5.4 Women's Safety Schemes

DERBY

The aim of each scheme is to empower women through self-protection and assertiveness training. As fear of violence and low self-esteem are addressed, women are able to access learning opportunities. Schemes are local, daytime, free, accessible, with childcare; signposting to educational opportunities is given.

For many women it is not merely a lack of confidence that prevents them from going back to learning or work, but fear. Fear of violence in the home or in the street can result in women staying at home more and more. At the same time their self-esteem falls even lower and a cycle of isolation and discouragement is set up.

Women's Safety Schemes were first begun in 1992 to address the needs of women who are fearful for whatever reason. Women workers from adult education and social services recognised that many women with whom they had contact could not access learning opportunities in their area because of fear. Some had been assaulted at some time by a partner, a stranger or a parent. Others were lacking confidence because of other traumatic events in their lives. Many wanted to start learning but were afraid to go out.

Course design

Transferability

The schemes have been designed to be flexible and easily transferable to other learning contexts. They have, so far, been delivered in a community context targeting women who have had little recent experience of learning.

Schemes could also be delivered as part of an access course or alongside any type of Return to Work/Learning course. Each scheme can be tailored to the needs of the target group and can take account of any special needs.

Courses have been set up integrating women who have been labelled as having learning difficulties, women with mental ill-health and women whose first language is not English.

Other possible contexts for the schemes could be work with the probation or prison service, or with police and victim support.

Progression

For many women, safety schemes are their first access point to education. Few will have any future educational plans for themselves. Taking part in and completing these courses very often begins to change these assumptions.

A considerable amount of effort is spent in pre-course outreach and publicity. Other local workers, e.g. health and social workers, may encourage women to join the courses. Other women will choose to come themselves. For many, coming along on the first day is a huge and terrifying step.

As the course progresses women grow in confidence and realise how much they have learnt. Towards the end of the course a guidance session is held. By this stage many women have discovered that they enjoy learning and have begun thinking about what they want to do next.

Where possible they can be referred to other courses in the area or to other providers (e.g. a local college). When specific courses cannot be found, adult community education tries to put on such courses.

On completing the Safety Scheme, participants receive a course certificate. It is planned that these courses be developed as an accredited course through the local Open College Network.

Curriculum

The aim of setting up a scheme rather than a course specifically for self-protection alone was to provide a combination of elements that contribute to women's safety.

The 'curriculum mix' has been experimental and has been improved with each new scheme. Research into attacks and attackers has shown that assertive behaviour will make a woman less likely to be a victim. We have experimented with various combinations of sessions, either alternating self-protection and assertiveness or interspersing assertiveness training into a predominantly self-protection course. Where assertiveness was only an occasional session the students have asked for more, as it does prove to be effective in making women feel safer.

We have also included a specific guidance session, providing information about other options for learning or training. A follow-up meeting a few weeks after the course has sometimes been arranged to continue discussions.

Language support has also been a new dimension in recent schemes. Students have interpretation into community languages and ESOL support throughout each session. Publicity is translated and course materials are translated or simplified.

The content of courses for women from other cultures has a particular emphasis on language needs. Extra time is built into these courses to give women more space to discuss concepts that are alien to their cultures (e.g. assertiveness, retaliation). More time is given for in-depth discussion and role play. Subjects such as racial harassment are dealt with. There is a discussion about the language needed to be safer and more confident in all kinds of situations.

Teaching the course

Since these courses combine two main elements – assertiveness and self-protection – it is important for tutors to be both skilled and experienced in teaching their own subject area and able to work with each other in order to produce an effective course. The tutors and the co-ordinator must also have an understanding of the issues affecting the women attending the course. Tutors need to have a full appreciation of their colleague's subject area. To achieve this, each is required to participate in the other tutor's sessions. This arrangement also helps to develop the course team. The co-ordinator/support tutor takes part in all the sessions.

Careful pre-course planning is necessary. At the same time tutors need to be flexible and responsive to the needs and concerns of the students as these emerge during the course itself. A valuable weekly feedback hour after each session provides an opportunity to do this. Team teaching of this kind does demand more of tutors, and communication must be open, clear and effective.

The courses are practical and are delivered in an informal and supportive way. The emphasis is on encouraging women to talk from their own experiences and feelings. Where hand-outs are necessary, they have to be kept simple and as clear as possible. They should also be presented in context and never in isolation. Since at least one member of staff will have ABE experience, the literacy needs of women can be identified and appropriate referrals made.

The needs of women with learning difficulties and those with disabilities or special needs must always be considered. Appropriate substitutes for hand-outs can be found, e.g. recording information on to audio tape for blind students and liaising with the support worker for women with learning difficulties.

The issues surrounding women's safety, domestic violence, etc. are clearly very difficult. Aware of this, one member of staff on each course has a background in general counselling and can attend to any women who may become distressed during the course or who may seek advice.

Staff development

We began the first scheme with staff using the traditional adult education tutor job descriptions. As a team, we had few pre-conceived ideas about how roles would develop. Gradually staff have created specific roles for the scheme that can combine in various ways with the delivery of the subjects. Thus, new job descriptions have emerged, forged by the staff through feedback, discussion and supervision sessions for roles such as co-ordinator, support tutor and language support. Team teaching has also developed each tutor's knowledge of other aspects of safety training, and tutors have welcomed this opportunity of training for themselves.

Supervision for staff has become an essential part of the scheme. It is especially important where new tutors are joining a team or when a tutor is taking on a new role.

Further training implications

A great number of different groups both in Derby and across the county are keenly interested in running such schemes. There are a number of developments that need to be made if such a growth is to happen. A forum or network is being formed in Derby to address the need for more suitably trained staff, a nationally recognised qualification in self-protection training and to address future funding issues. The forum will also attempt to raise the profile of this area of work.

Monitoring and evaluation

It has been necessary to monitor the progress of the schemes and evaluate their effectiveness. The Derby Safer Cities project, the main funder, requires this, and reports have been needed too for the participating partners: Community Education and Social Services. Formal and informal monitoring and evaluation has been conducted throughout.

Valuable information gathered demonstrates that the original aims and objectives of the courses were met. At the same time areas requiring improvement or further development have been highlighted.

5.5.5 Women's Self Defence Training the Trainers Course

WEA BRISTOL WOMEN'S BRANCH

Background

A steering group of women workers and volunteers in the Bristol voluntary and statutory sectors had been meeting together since 1991. Members of the group brought with them a wealth of experience of working with women in the community and all had separately identified a clear need for Women's Self Defence courses and a severe shortage of suitably qualified women instructors.

The Group made contact with organisers and tutors from other Self Defence Training the Trainers projects in the UK. A philosophy and possible structure for a course was identified and local accreditation was negotiated. The ultimate objective is to obtain national accreditation, through the Royal Society of Arts (RSA) as at present no qualification exists specifically for 'Women's Self Defence'.

It had been identified that most courses organised in the local Bristol area were based on one or other martial art and were taught by male instructors. Experience within the steering group showed that this approach, on its own, does not necessarily meet the needs of women and can leave them feeling more vulnerable than before.

The steering group's aim was to train approximately 16 women self defence instructors in a recognised and validated course. These women would then be able to pass on their knowledge and skills to women from all walks of life in youth and community centres, schools, village halls, workplaces and sports centres throughout the area. We are particularly keen to make this opportunity available to women who are traditionally under-represented in sporting activities, for example older women, many younger women and disabled women.

Accreditation of the course has been sought through the RSA Customer Specific Scheme in order to develop a nationally recognised standard for the teaching of women's self defence.

The course was managed, supported and monitored by a steering group made up of interested representatives from voluntary and statutory bodies. The group of women qualified as self defence trainers have formed a network for ongoing support.

Aims

The primary aim of the course is to enable a diverse group of women from different communities in Bristol to be able to pass on self defence skills to other women.

The course recognised that self defence is about having choices – even in frightening situations. A self defence class should enable the students to have confidence in their individual skills, strategies and resources, and these can include:

- a knowledge of the basic principles of fighting such that the student can adapt/invent according to the context and to her abilities
- an appreciation of her own ability to be creative and flexible in situations in the use of interpersonal skills – humour, calmness and kindness as well as avoidance, assertion and anger.

All the techniques and related material should be taught and addressed with regard to a clear anti-racist and anti-sexist perspective.

The training course took into account the following guiding principles:

- any self defence course needs to be fun and enjoyable as a physical activity in its own right
- women already have skills and experience that can be brought to bear on their own defence
- the ability to generate techniques that are appropriate for an individual woman is more important than learning set sequences
- students wishing to learn self defence are not necessarily fit, young or able
- self-esteem is an essential element in a woman's ability to effectively defend herself
- a substantial and well-supported group of women's self defence teachers will be a firm basis from which to offer a programme of self defence courses within the community, thus having a significant impact on women's vulnerability.

Objectives

To give women attending the Training the Trainers course the opportunity to:

- experience and evaluate a self defence course
- learn a variety of self defence skills
- learn how to teach a physical activity in an enjoyable and safe way with particular reference to an awareness of fitness and health
- learn about different teaching/learning methods and the way in which adults learn and demonstrate their skills in a practice teaching situation
- explore issues relating to women's vulnerability
- learn from each other's knowledge and experience
- gain confidence as potential teachers of self defence
- develop supports and contacts to assist them in future work.

Recruitment

The course was widely advertised through community networks and local media. Twenty-two women were originally recruited; 15 of them stayed the course and gained the qualification.

Support funding was also secured so that we were able to support three disabled women to train as trainers, one of whom is deaf and for whom we were able to provide a BSL interpreter and a notetaker.

Support funding also allowed us to pay childcare expenses to enable women with children to attend the course. An accessible venue was hired. The course has a concessionary fee policy.

Students were supported throughout by the trainers. Individual and group tutorials formed part of the course and participants' emotional needs were addressed as part of the course philosophy.

Course content

The course comprised three stages:

Stage One

A self defence course for the trainees, including thorough learning of techniques and plenty of time for discussion and evaluation.

Stage Two

Part A: Time to explore issues such as:

- racism
- the law
- rape
- domestic violence
- differences between women and implications for working with different groups.

Part B: Teaching styles and groupwork methods, including elements such as: planning, adults as learners, trainer's role, games, warm-ups, problems in classes, how to handle disclosures, resources, evaluation.

Stage Three

Teaching practice with the trainee group. The course content and methods were negotiated and evaluated with the trainees throughout.

Evaluation

Since the course was run as a pilot for the RSA Women's Self Defence Training of Trainers, a thorough evaluation of the process and outcomes is about to begin. Quantitative data has been compiled throughout the duration of the course and some qualitative evaluation has already taken place with the successful participants.

Evaluation and monitoring methods used will provide both qualitative and quantitative information – for example, student profile, attendance records, student feedback and personal learning records, records of content of sessions, observation by outside evaluators.

Chapter 6

Some Questions and Conclusions

The extracts in the three previous chapters demonstrate that there is a wide range of educational and training provision available to women, at least in some parts of the country. The extracts also indicate that this provision is of a high standard and designed to meet the needs of the various groups of women concerned.

Although it has to be recognised that the submissions received cannot be seen as representative of the overall pattern of provision for women, certain trends are evident. This enables us to frame some questions as well as draw some conclusions:

- is provision for women increasing as more institutions and organisations see women as an appropriate target group for expansion?
- is that provision consistently of a high standard and informed by the criteria of good practice?
- are funding requirements making the provision less flexible and less responsive by prescribing the outcomes?
- has the imposition of accreditation altered the collective, supportive nature of much provision for women?
- have funding requirements affected the range of provision available by encouraging more vocationally-oriented provision?
- have the funding requirements encouraged the expansion of provision which limits the choices of many women and directs them into low paid, low status work?
- is the threshold provision which is community-based, non-threatening and not accredited being reduced because it may not qualify for funding?

That these questions need to be asked is a cause for concern.

But the picture presented by the extracts, and indeed by all the responses, is also encouraging:

- diverse good practice does exist; adapting to external constraints need not mean compromise
- innovation and creativity can be seen in many types of provision
- the need for support and for appropriate progression is clearly recognised and provided
- women in under-represented groups and those that are particularly disadvantaged are being encouraged and enabled to participate
- evaluation that leads to development is thorough and involves the women concerned.

The WEPC hopes that by disseminating the information we received, by sharing examples of good practice but also raising areas of concern, we are contributing to the maintenance and indeed the expansion of appropriate educational and training opportunities for women. We hope that we are emphasising the need for guidelines to good practice through the examples included in this book. We are also aware of the need to observe the warning signs and to challenge policies which threaten to reduce or remove the range of opportunities available. Above all we hope that these extracts will help others to adapt, to develop and to create provision which retains the essential characteristics, meets the criteria and becomes recognisable as examples of good practice.

APPENDIX 1

Submissions for the Award

Title of the provision and by whom the submission was made, listed in order of receipt by NIACE.

Bridgend College Day Care Consultancy
Bridgend College of Further and Higher Education

New Start for Women
William Newton FE Centre, Stockton-on-Tees

Parent Introductory Course
Bournville College of Further Education

Introduction to Women's Studies
Doncaster College

South Glamorgan Women's Workshop
Cardiff

Access to the Childcare and Education NVQ
Dan-y-Coed Education and Training Services

Women's Resource and Development Agency
Belfast

Fair Play Training and Development Project
Mid-Craigie, Dundee

Return to Study Skills for Women
Gorseinon College

Trevethin Young Mothers Project
Gwent Tertiary College

Making Headway Programme
Careers Research and Advisory Centre, Cambridge

Courses in the Clerical Department
Cottingham Adult Education Centre, Hull

Women's Self-defence Training the Trainers Course
WEA Bristol Women's Branch

Access Programme (Women Only Routes)
Huddersfield Technical College

Enterprising Women
WEA Highland, Inverness

Business Skills Update
Mid-Kent College of Further and Higher Education

Pathways for Women Returners
Llandrillo College, Clwyd

Women Returners – Information Technology
City of Liverpool Community College

Training for Work
Presceli Training Centre

Skills for Women Project
Harehills ex-Middle School, Leeds

Classroom Assistant Training
Mid-Kent College of Further and Higher Education

Women's Guidance Project
Nelson and Colne College

Fresh Start Women's Access Course
The Sheffield College

Women's Motor Vehicle Course
Castle Centre, Sheffield College

Women into Office Administration and New Technology
Doncaster College

English for Speakers of Other Languages (ESOL)
Marsh Centre, Huddersfield Technical College

Women's Safety Schemes
Derby East Adult Community Education Team

Women, Work, Skills
WEA Leicester

Women on the Move
Surrey Adult Continuing Education

Women: Time for a Change
WEA Northern District

Abertillery Young Mothers Project
Gwent Tertiary College

Returning to Work, Further Education or Training
Nene Valley Adult Education

Confidence Building for Women
Wearside College

Women and New Directions
Craigroyston Community High School, Edinburgh

Brush Up Your English and Maths
WEA East Midlands District

Childwise
Calderdale Associates, Halifax

AWAAZ Asian Women's Training Project
Roshni Asian Women's Centre

Access for Women into Art
Kent Adult Education, Gillingham

Women Mean Business
Devon Community Development Agency

Selby ALBSU Partnership
The Cygnet Centre, Selby

Women's Course Programme
Barnsley College

MaTReC NVQ Embedding Project
Manor Training and Resource Centre, Sheffield

Giving Real Opportunities to Women (GROW)
Rother Valley College

Women into Electrical Installations and Plumbing
Dollis Hill Centre, College of North West London

Women's Retraining Projects
Rother Valley College

Life Skills Rhondda
Hafod Primary School, Mid Glamorgan

New Start/Starting Again
Suffolk West Federation of Women's Institutes

Women Only Business Course
Elephant Enterprises, London

Trekkers Travel Club
The Power House, Cardiff

Science and Technology Taster Course for Women
North Tyneside College

Women Returners' Skills Update
Canterbury College

Outreach Programme – Bilingual Work with Asian Women
Department of Continuing Education, Lancaster University

Improve your Skills – English and Numeracy
Farnborough College of Technology

Wider Opportunities for Women
Farnborough College of Technology

APL Project
Hackney Community College

New Start
Saxmundham Middle School, Suffolk

Abertillery Young Parents Project
Abertillery Community Education Centre

Women's Education in Building
Construction Skills Training Centre, London

Women in the Workforce: Alternative Choices for Women from Coalmining areas
DOVE Workshop, Neath

WEA Margaret Saunders Branch
WEA Thames and Solent District

Craigneuk and Petersburn Women Writers Workshop
Petersburn Library, Airdrie

Women Returners
Kent Adult Education Service

Women into Work
South Leeds Open Learning Centre

Faculty of Education and Community Studies
University of Reading

Women Returners: Accounts/Legal
Stourbridge College

Openings for Women
Bradford Language Scheme, Bradford and Ilkley Community College

Rutland, Melton and Vale of Belvoir Women's Access Project
Melton Mowbray College

Accreditation in the Community
WEA Bristol Women's Branch

Risca Outreach Project – Women's Return to Learn
Risca, Gwent

The Valleys Women's Roadshow
Risca, Gwent

Certificate for Mature Students – Women's Route
Department of General Education, Bradford and Ilkley Community College

APPENDIX 2

Acronyms

ABE	Adult Basic Education
AP(E)L	Accreditation of Prior (Experiential) Learning
BSL	British Sign Language
BTEC	Business and Technology Education Council
C&G	City and Guilds of London Institute
CAB	Citizens Advice Bureau
CLAIT	Computer Literacy and Information Technology
CREW	Centre for Research on European Women
DFEE	Department for Education and Employment
EC	European Commission
ESF	European Social Fund
ESOL	English for Speakers of Other Languages
FEFC	Further Education Funding Council
GNVQ	General National Vocational Qualification
HEFC	Higher Education Funding Council
LEA	Local Education Authority
LEC	Local Enterprise Company
LOCN	Leicestershire Open College Network
NEAB	Northern Examinations and Assessment Board
NEBSM	National Examining Board in Supervisory Management
NNEB	National Nursery Examination Board
NOW	New Opportunities for Women

NVQ	National Vocational Qualification
OCN	Open College Network
RSA	Royal Society of Arts
SCOTVEC	Scottish Vocational and Educational Council
SVQ	Scottish Vocational Qualification
SYOCF	South Yorkshire Open College Federation
TEC	Training and Enterprise Council
TOCF	Tyneside Open College Federation
WEA	Workers' Educational Association
WNYAN	West and North Yorkshire Access Network

APPENDIX 3

References

Coats, M. (1994) *Women's Education*, Open University Press and SRHE.

McGivney, V. (1993) *Women's Education and Training: Barriers to access, informal starting points and progression routes*, NIACE.

NIACE (1994) *Women Learning: Ideas, approaches and practical support*.